No One's
Business

No One's Business

Business

A migrant's barefoot journey to millions

Vadim Turcanu

No One's Business by Vadim Turcanu

Copyright © 2017 by Vadim Turcanu

ISBN: 978-1-9997259-0-7 (softcover)
ISBN: 978-1-9997259-1-4 (hardcover)
ISBN: 978-1-9997259-2-1 (ebook)
ISBN: 978-1-9999346-2-0 (audiobook)

Book design by Sun Editing & Book Design, www.suneditwrite.com

Published by Picassic Limited
40A Warwick Way, London, SW1V 1RY

Printed and bound in the United Kingdom

This book is dedicated to my parents and family, who have always put me in a place that motivates me to do more; to my coach, Philip Batir, for his faith in me and the opportunity he has given me; to my LIRPS coach, Vasile Luca, who gave me a strong start with his stern approach, which made me a stronger man; to my friends, starting from LIRPS, who have been with me in the toughest situations during the early years of my development; and to my wife and son, who gave me my soft, loving side and reason to change.

I would like to give thanks to all those with a big heart who have helped me throughout the journey; to Marina Nani, for her appearance at the right time and her push and support; and to Viktoria Cerena, who worked tirelessly at night at various stages in the creation of this book.

CONTENTS

FOREWORD

ACCORDING TO THE LATEST migration report by the UN, there are 244 million migrants worldwide, with an additional 5 million reaching out for new shores every year. Rising international migration is the new reality in every corner of the globe and a red flag for a potential social divide in the Western countries, where more than two-thirds of all international migrants are seeking peace and prosperity.

We could all play the blame game and think that the airlines made it too easy, cheap and fast for people to uproot themselves and move to a better city, to a better country, for a better lifestyle. But what compels people to leave their home and old life to pursue the dream of a better life?

The world is a wonderful place is only true for some of us, for others it is a harsh reality of conflicts, lack of opportunities, poverty and social inequality. What makes you leave everything you know, everyone you love behind and trade them for a better future for yourself and your family?

The number of migrants to middle-income countries is declining but rising to high-income countries. What is the story behind these high-achieving migrants who take the world by storm with their brilliance, passion for fast results and compassion? What is the untold story?

In *No One's Business*, a courageous young man from Moldova walks for six months to reach a destination he knows nothing about, a new country where even prison is a better option than what he left behind. Vadim Turcanu is a world-class entrepreneur, judo champion and philanthropist who shares his own vision to create better life choices.

As the author shares his true story—walking barefoot for six months with nothing but his own dream to be a winner at the game of life—some people could think, "Why do I need to know his story?" The answer is very simple: You can learn who you are, and how to overcome limiting beliefs and social conditioning. But the key message of this book is that you are a migrant yourself, even if you have never left your comfortable home looking for a better life. Even when you have achieved what was expected of you, you still have the right to be curious about who you are, and what is available when you open your mind to other people's realities. What have they done to be so successful?

Migration is not about geography, and is not strictly about moving from a village to a city, from one country to another, but about moving from where you are in your life at present to where you want to be.

Marina Nani, Founder, Radio W.O.R.K.S. World

1

MIGRATION

I HAVE NO IDEA whether it is night or it's still day. I forgot to ask what time it was when I left.

The wind blows into my face and ruffles my hair. The street noise is much sharper, the ear-tickling roar of the car engines, and I can almost feel the exhaust fumes touching my face.

I left a meeting at the Park Plaza hotel in Victoria and am going to Victoria station to get the Tube home. It's been a long time since I last used the Tube—and it's certainly very different from the experience of driving home, which I've been used to for the past six years.

Just this time it is more than unusual: I cannot see. I am not sure where I am most of the time and I am being guided by an eight-year-old. I wouldn't normally allow an eight-year-old to go by himself to the park by the house, let alone guide an adult around London ....

I trust my son, but he is only eight! It is the second day I haven't been able to see. We've got lost at least three times,

11

including around the house. I cannot believe how lost I am in terms of navigation. Although I'm told where I stand and what am I facing, I am not able to imagine the location without visual cues. Relying on my son, Alex, for guidance, although not perfect, has managed to keep me alive for almost two days. I have to constantly reassure him and tell him to alert me if there are any steps, trees or walls, just in case his mind drifts and he forgets to inform me. I've already got a light bruise on my shoulder and had a couple of tree branches smack me in the face—it's understandable, Alex is much shorter and the low branches do not reach him.

I've had to cancel a couple of meetings and conduct them by phone instead as I could have only made them on time by driving.

The fact that I cannot check my phone for feeds, text messages and emails is playing on my nerves.

There is almost nothing I can do without someone's assistance. And this feels crazy, as I have never been reliant on someone for something.

I'm regretting even starting this experiment.

After conducting my first interview on my radio show, I had envisaged interviewing Oleg Cretul. Oleg is an important person in my life. Unknowingly, he has always motivated me. While he has been in the darkest places of anyone I know—at just twenty-one, he lost everything he had and valued most in a tragic car accident, his wife, his unborn child and his eyes—he's managed to stand up and go on to become a husband, a father and a Paralympic judo champion. He is also the most positive and uplifting person I know. That is something I greatly admire and am moved by.

But how would I do this? It was relatively easy to find Oleg's number but would he talk to me? Would he accept the request? Was my radio show, with so far only one other interview, worthy to invite such a man? A true man and a true champion. And here I come with my little radio show. How would his denial affect my self-esteem and my new venture? I had only started and had zero experience in the interview field. I'd be rubbish at it and he would just tell me to fuck off! Shit, I'm not doing it!

But I had a chance. I had always used my chances, so I had to this time too.

My palms were sweating and my heartbeats were probably being heard by the hotel barman who was fifty-nine feet away.

It had been twenty minutes since Oleg's coach, Vitaly Gligor, had kindly given me Oleg's number and I was still hesitating to call.

My mind was full of doubts, fear of rejection and loud, discomfiting noise.

It's just a call, nothing will happen, only a bloody call!

I was battling with myself. I had to reassure my monkey mind that I was worthy, that I was ready, that I could do it, and should he turn me down, I could try again.

"Monkey mind" is an expression describing the moment when your thoughts run uncontrollably. It's when you try to meditate, sleep or concentrate on one thing and various unrelated thoughts just come in without you being able to control or stop them.

There was nothing real, just my own thoughts but it all felt like a real battle.

I realised that I was my only enemy! It was now forty minutes since I'd got the number, and I hadn't talked to Oleg only because I was busy battling with myself. There was nothing real, only my thoughts were keeping me from ringing him up.

"Oleg, hi, this is Vadim Turick..." I used my nickname from the old days, and proceeded to explain who I was in a hasty voice without letting him respond.

"Yes, I know," he interrupted me. "What's needed?"

In under a minute, he'd accepted and we'd agreed the day and time.

This is so amazing! I feel like I've won the lottery! Bloody hell, all this thinking and I only needed to call!

What happened to me happens to a lot to people. A thought had got to my mind. And some people never decide to make that call, as there is just no way to convince the monkey mind that you are ready or worthy for your *big* idea.

Now I had to prepare for the interview. I looked at my questions and they didn't satisfy me. Marina (my partner in Radio W.O.R.K.S. World) sent me a new set of questions that were better but still I was uneasy.

The next day, I was flying to Spain for business, and while on the plane, I had this idea: If I covered my eyes and experienced a day of his life, the questions should come by themselves. It was a eureka moment. It felt like the million-dollar idea.

While on the plane, the idea started developing, but it opened a can of worms, of questions and conversations with myself.

If I spend only one day being blindfolded, that would be rather easy. However, it might not prompt any useful questions for the interview, especially if the day I choose is at the weekend.

OK, I'll take two days—one at the weekend and one work-day. That should prepare me well and give me at least a little understanding of his daily life.

I envisaged me walking with someone with something covering my eyes and people following me with their gaze. Some people would think, "What's this guy about? What is he doing with that thing on his eyes?"

I would attract attention. Attention means eyeballs. And eyeballs in business means people and people are customers and customers are money.

A chain of thoughts started. *OK, so I could advertise my business or the radio, or even better, the radio show. And even better, this particular interview.*

What else was possible? I could raise some money for charity. But what charity? I had no idea how it worked. Certainly, if I hung a can around my neck, it wouldn't be much of a success. But there were lots of guys doing various things for charity. How did they do it? I decided to start researching it as soon as I got wifi.

I was only in Spain for a couple of days and had quite a lot to do and no time to think or research during the day, so I only got down to reading when I got back to my hotel (and its wifi) in the evening.

I read everything I could find about raising money for charity. And just before 2 a.m., I found a good and appro-priate cause—fundraising for the National Eye Research Centre.

I set everything up with all the information and a description of my idea, pledged some funds from my side towards the target amount, then shared this with friends on Facebook and went to sleep.

When I woke in the morning, I was a little in shock and my head was spinning a bit. *Shit, how will I do this?* I had a business to run. I had meetings scheduled. How would I get to the meetings if I couldn't drive? Who could I get to drive my car and guide me? Would I even be able to find someone at this short notice? I had so much to do in Spain and would only get back to London on Saturday evening, which would not give me time to prepare anything.

Well, I guess the questions I thought this would prompt have started appearing.

I began logging in to my account thinking that perhaps I could postpone the whole thing for a few days.

I recently listened to a great interviewer who said that he had such fear before every interview that he hoped that the guest would call and decline so he would not need to do it. That was the exact feeling I had at this time.

But when I logged in, I saw that some of friends had already pledged money and half of the target amount was already raised. There was surely no way back now.

All the preparation I managed to do during my busy schedule in Spain was to ask my assistant to buy two large white T-shirts. I envisaged writing a link to the donation page on the T-shirt so if someone wanted to contribute, they could just take a picture of the link and do it. I didn't plan to make a big deal of it but just give an opportunity for someone who decided to help.

Now I was thinking how I could properly cover my eyes, so I would be *completely* blind for forty-eight hours. Also,

the thought of who would be my guide was slightly bothering me. I didn't know anyone that would be available.
Everyone was at work, at school, and so on. What had I got
myself into?

I had to at least figure something out to cover my eyes.
My friend Slavik had a good meditation mask, but it was
usually in use, and in any case, let the light through.

Then I had an idea.

As soon as I landed in London, I rushed into Soho.
I've never before run to find a sex shop! When you are
not looking for one, there is a sex shop at every corner in
Soho, but, of course, when you're looking for something
specific... But after spending quite a bit of time, I found
an appropriate eye mask. I also thought to tape my eyes to
prevent myself from opening them by accident.

The first friend I asked to guide me had to decline
due to a flight and all the others I knew were busy. After
much consideration, I decided my son, Alex, was the best
option. So we went for it and I took him out of school
for a day. I also decided to create a little video about
this experience, which can be found online with the tag
ConsciouslyBlind.

Although there have been frustrations coming from
comforts being taken away, these two days without sight
have revealed something important—something that might
have taken years to learn or realise.

Over the years, I've learned many things, studied many
people and read many books. And it's all been great—but
it's all about the road, the path. Yet, as the famous quote
goes, "There are just two big moments in someone's life: the

day you were born and the day you found out why." And while I had been looking to build my "road" through intensive learning and personal development, it has been during this ConsciouslyBlind experiment that I've stumbled on the destination. I've realised how beautiful the world is if you just shut up and listen.

When I reply to people helping me or asking me questions, my answer is purely addressing their soul—bypassing their external appearance.

Every bit of food I chew is relished by my taste buds and stomach. The flavour is overwhelming. Without all the external distractions, it is as if I am tasting for the first time. The meal becomes a transcendent experience, like a ritual or an enthralling act in some gustatory theatre.

I can imagine anything I want from things I touch and hear without the imposition of visual reality.

In this state, I find my level of trust towards people rises—and it is funny how people change for the better if they feel trusted. It creates a great vibe between who you are and who you interact with.

And, most importantly, walking blindfold for forty-eight hours minded by my eight-year-old son has been the most uninterrupted time I've ever spent with him. This blindfold experience has opened my eyes to something I have never seen before. I've actually started seeing! It has been astonishing to realise his maturity and responsibility for those close to him. I had been too busy with my daily activities to closely observe his big heart.

I realise that when present, here and now, you see you are surrounded by the best people in the world.

It is also an achievement to realise just how unimportant we are to most people and how few people care for us or wake up with us in mind. It is a door to creativity, fearlessness and great achievement. There is no fear of looking stupid or being wrong—and all that is new and great comes from the unknown, from numerous tries, failures and embarrassment. It is summed up in this quote often attributed to Gandhi:

> *First they will ignore us, then they will laugh at us,*
> *then they will try to fight us, then we win.*

Or put another way: *It is amazing what you can accomplish if you don't care who gets the credit.* I read it somewhere, I've tried it and it works.

MIGRATION MEANS CHANGE

> *Change is hard at first, messy in the middle*
> *and gorgeous at the end.*
> —Robin Sharma

Well, whatever happens, migration is always an option. Change from where you are to where you want to be—from one mindset to another and from one circumstance to another. If life doesn't bring you happiness—migrate!

We are all migrants—of geography, social position or mindset. There are no people that do not "migrate", as migration is a process of change and growth. Unfortunately, a lot of the time people have the wrong attitude—towards geographical migrants particularly.

Remember when you went to school or nursery for the first time as a kid? You didn't know anyone there and you were away from the parents you loved. Well, this was almost exactly what I felt like as I migrated across Europe to Britain—plus, I had neither any knowledge of the languages or useful skills.

I was born in part of the USSR that, five years after my birth, became the Republic of Moldova. My family was humble, middle class (speaking in current English terms) and we lived in a medium-sized village. We just washed our faces in the morning and feet in the evening—if they were dirty. It was normal to have a bath only once a week. There was no running water, so my parents would heat some water and we would take turns to wash in the same tub—from the youngest to the eldest. It seems crazy now, but it was completely normal at the time. Moldova is a wonderful country with ancient traditions. The people are very friendly and happy. We have great writers and folk singers that touch the heart, the famous *hora* circle dance, and many delicious national dishes. We have one of the best and most fruitful soils in Europe, which produces unmissable tasty fruit and vegetables. The wines are amazing—the best I have ever tasted anywhere. And achievements in the sports arena, considering the size of the country, are impressive.

However, the country, after winning independence from the Soviet Union in 1991, was badly hit by various economic crises to such an extent that by the late 1990s, every second family had someone working abroad: a mother, father, brother or sister. People were leaving their homes, partners and kids, which often broke the family bonds and resulted in divorces and lost children.

Of course, most of the people could not afford, or were not qualified enough, to just go abroad for work. The majority couldn't obtain a Schengen visa, so the solution was to get a tourist visa to a neighbouring EU country and work illegally by overstaying the visa.

And if you couldn't get a visa, you had to try another way. The commonest was just crossing the border to the neighbouring EU country, usually by foot, sometimes hidden in a train or over a river in an inflatable boat, all the time avoiding the border police. But even when you crossed the border and reached the target country, there was a big chance that you would be reported by the locals to the border police. In these areas, local people were vigilantly looking for signs of illegal "tourists" to report them, often for a reward. So crossing the border was only one step. There was still a large risk of being sent back to the country you crossed from, if you did not move quickly and cautiously, or did not have a strong enough plan.

Though the border crossing was a very stressful, challenging and often life-threatening journey, still there were quite a lot of people going for it in desperation, even when they had families back home. They walked through the woods or fields, in hopefully the right direction, often with no clear route or coordination, enduring hunger and starvation. The majority of these people had taken high-interest loans from sharks, so there was no way back unless they could find the money to pay the interest.

There was a belief at the time that when anyone left the country to live abroad anywhere in Europe that their life would be great—work, no struggles for survival, all your basic needs provided for. Well, technically that was true, although you could feel the price people paid for it, and the quality of life outside of working hours wasn't always something you would agree had made it all worthwhile.

Imagine you had been dropped off in an unknown country with no understanding of the local language or any sort of foreign language. You were among a group of people that had survived in the jungle. You were equipped with high survival and navigation skills and a good knowledge of bird and monkey languages but not plumbing, forex trading or Excel. And you all arrive in a big city seeking to settle and get a job. There are people in these circumstances every day. Luckily, the majority are able to find a way, and you hear them talking later about how they learned the language, found work and what life feels like in a new country.

The strong motivation to survive drives you beyond limits you never before thought possible.

If you didn't "walk" to another country, there were other routes—especially if you were one of those "fortunate" people who could afford to pay. It was a common thing for a professional organisation to go abroad, such as a sports team for a tournament, while half of them were unrelated to that profession. They were only there for transit purposes, having paid to be transported abroad. It was not rare for the *whole team* to be fake. Quite a few managers and federations were only staying afloat as a result of this human trafficking. In the early 2000s, I was training as a judoka and fairly sure that any financial support I received mainly came from this source too.

However, since it was a result of circumstances, I felt there was no immoral tag attached to it. It was similar to when we look back in history and see inhuman activity that was considered as normal at the time—simply the realities of the country in question during the period referred to. The whole set up was mutually beneficial for all the parties involved: those who paid to be fake sportspeople got an opportunity to go abroad for a better life; and for the organisers and professionals it provided the opportunity to demonstrate their skills abroad and earn funds that were not provided by the government.

Also, it was quite common for the actual sportspeople to go to an overseas tournament then abandon the team and go off to settle abroad—with their home country losing more talent. As I was in the sporting field, I knew of guys teaching their skills, often very successfully, in almost every country of the EU.

Like nature and evolution, the market shapes itself by creating various forms. The list of jobs the people found themselves doing abroad was rather narrow, due to the lack of the local language and skill requirements. Where "we" came from we did not have the same skill sets. (People educated in the USSR were trained for jobs that mostly just did not exist in the EU.)

We don't live to think—we think in order to survive successfully.

And once they were abroad, almost everyone, regardless of their day (or night) job, was shoplifting food and household goods or stealing in public places, toilets or libraries—anything unguarded would be taken with no remorse whatsoever. One could say that they were a breed of parasites with no human feelings, but my theory is that we grew up in a communist society where nothing belonged to anyone in particular, and you could pick up whatever you liked as everything was common property. From a young age, I would bring home fruits and vegetables from the fields belonging to a *kolkhoz* (a Soviet-era collective farm). At the same time, everyone, including kids, would go and work for the same organisation for free, during harvest time.

With the "picking up of available goods" being quite common abroad, and there being more goods "available" than one could personally use, a black market evolved in those countries, where people would buy and sell the surplus stolen goods at half price.

Some people would make this their only purpose to go abroad—going for a short time, "picking up" and on returning, making rather substantial profits. The most common products became commodities as they were easy to sell, regardless of quantity and there was always a demand: motorcycles, car radios, cigarettes, razorblades, batteries, designer clothes, cars, motorboat engines, jewellery.

Usually, after a short time, most of people would integrate into the new community, get a job and never shoplift again. However, others would learn only after being imprisoned.

MAKING THE FIRST STEP—IMAGINE AND MAKE A DECISION

Stop looking for happiness in the same place you lost it.

I often remember one day in August 2003. I was aged nineteen and sitting on a bench by the monument of the Bulgarian nationalist poet Hristo Botev and looking at my old school, the Liceul Internat Republican cu Profil Sportiv, known as LIRPS. I had graduated from there the year before, then enrolled in the architecture faculty at the Technical University of Moldova, but only attended once. I hadn't enrolled because of any passion to be an architect, although drawing was my hobby, but mostly because the enrolment was easy—there was no entry exam. And they needed someone to represent the university in the sports arena.

Anyway, nothing had really changed since I graduated from LIRPS. I was still training there twice a day, six days a week. I felt as if I was still at LIRPS, and I hated myself for still hanging around there. I remembered how we used to laugh at those few guys that were still living in the accommodation and eating at the canteen—and now I was one of them.

Although I'd achieved great results in judo and was recognised as a good sportsman, most of the time I was broke. I had no money for bus travel and was always starving, lacking proper nutrition, and would eat anything and everything—as soon as I spied anything edible. The worst thing was that there were no prospects, nothing to aim for. I felt that I had already reached my goal and could not see another step up that would motivate me to push harder.

My sport didn't pay but I knew that I didn't want the life I had been living with my parents. I knew there had to be something better. Sitting on the bench, I was contemplating where this was all going, where I would be and how I would be living in a year's time—on exactly the same day, at the same time. I had a strong desire to change. Due to my sporting career, no other options seemed available, but the desire was immense.

I thought about the guys I'd heard about from LIRPS who were in prison in Europe for shoplifting. They'd initially gone for a tournament but then just broken away and escaped from the team to avoid returning to Moldova and instead stayed where they were for the "better opportunities". I had heard that the prisons were amazing—good food, TV and daily visits to gym. *Shit, this is better than my life now!* I thought. *Sounds perfect.* This seemed like one option. It wouldn't be too hard to get into prison if I somehow could make it into Europe.

Here I was, on this bench and looking down at my old flip-flops, feeling bad for myself but with the drums of change beating in my heart. They were so strong that I could feel them in my chest and I promised myself that this current life had got to end. The same thoughts had been in my mind a number of times in the past five months, but this time everything was so intense. You know when you have a dream and you feel everything as if it is real with all the visual and sensation details? That was how it felt.

From that moment, I began hating every detail and activity of my life.

The fear of never having a chance to change my life for the better—this was the fear that had been hidden inside me. I learned that this fear could serve as my drive and motivation to move ahead in spite of everything, to select the people I wanted to be with and be in control of the choices I made.

Your life does not get better by chance,
it gets better by change.
—Jim Rohn

If you find yourself trapped and your energy being drained in business, work, a friendship or relationship, it is time to change.

At the time of my editing this book, I started my radio show, *The Intelligent Migrant Show*, on Radio W.O.R.K.S. World. For a while, I'd felt some unease with what I was doing in my daily life and felt I needed a change. There is a saying that you attract what you think about. I think that you just start seeing differently once you see the opportunity—like when you buy a new car and suddenly you notice more cars like yours on the road. So I grabbed the opportunity to host a radio show right when it came to me—without thinking whether I have the right experience or skills or not. And actually I am quite bad—you can check out my interviews, I personally cannot stand my voice—but I am sure that without the practice I will never get better and without the change, nothing will change.

Further Reading: *Vagabonding,* Rolf Potts; *The 4-Hour Work Week,* Timothy Ferriss; *Who Moved My Cheese?* Spencer Johnson; *Our Iceberg Is Melting,* Holger Rathgeber and John Kotter; *The Tipping Point,* Malcolm Gladwell.

2

Identity

YOU ARE THE CREATOR of your identity. No one can create it but you. It's like the choices we make—it is us who must choose. No matter where you are coming from, what matters is where you want to *be*.

You cannot control anything in life and the best thing is to go with the flow and let shit unfold. Be open to a change of circumstances and use the opportunities those circumstances bring—what unfolds could be better than the original plan. The only thing you can control is how you respond.

WHY YOU ARE WHO YOU ARE

Is the frog green because it lives in greenish water or is the water green because of the frogs living there?

The green frogs have been more successful in camouflaging themselves from predators than those who had more visible colours. This is a proven fact and a vast number of evolutions and mutations in plants and animals have happened before our very eyes in only the past few decades. This has been either as an effect of the change of temperature and ecosystem or as an effect of human activity. A vivid example is the mouse that was recently discovered to have become immune to common rodent poison.

Changes and the environment affect us humans too. Our characters, our physiques and abilities are also adapting to the environment we grow up and live in, as well as the people we are surrounded with.

My theory is that in general all people are good. First, the child is happy and playful and he or she is taught to respect those surrounding him or her. Apart from rare cases of extreme environments, all humans are brought up with similar principles and philosophy. But the environment, influential people and later circumstances change the person as he or she adapts to those surroundings and aims to survive and succeed in them. Remember the story of Mowgli from the *Jungle Book*? (And there are actual cases of people who have survived and lived in the wild, without transforming into a monster.) Unlike unforgiving nature, if humans are willing to try to adapt to new circumstances and survive, even thrive in them, then, I believe, they will have an extremely positive approach to adapting to *any* process of change.

There is no opportunity for change in a world in which you feel comfortable, so it takes a desire to get out of the comfort zone to bring about change and find new opportunities. You have to be willing to be uncomfortable if you want to change your life for the better—I sometimes call it being "eagerly uncomfortable".

And there is an opportunity in every person or place that you pass by. With all the news that you read and hear, and in everything you say, how do you know what is the correct path, or the one that will lead you to your desired outcome? Well, we would be extremely bored if we knew all the answers all of the time—we just cannot live without surprises! So we follow the more usual practice of trial and error. With that, of course, will come both big successes and huge mistakes—it's called evolution... nature. Think of the sperm fighting to reach the womb, what were the chances that *you* would be born?

The fact that you are born is already a miracle!

The survival instinct is so powerful that it shapes everything and performs wonders. Imagine being held underwater and not being able to breathe. Your oxygen reserves are exhausting and your muscular contractions are getting stronger, with increasing frequency... finally, you manage to escape and get your head above water for that deep, critical breath of air, which you needed more than anything. It is that sort of desire that I am referring to.

Who we are is a product of our past circumstances,
but our future is shaped by our choices.

In the mid-1990s, as a child, I looked in admiration whenever I saw strong champions—proud and glorious as they raised their national flags around the world, demonstrating their work and achievement. It felt that nothing would be in their way and they had the whole world at their feet. These moments always drove me, giving me the desire to achieve and the motivation to get results.

As a child, like a hungry stray dog jumping at a piece of meat thrown at it, I gulped down all the judo techniques that the coach would demonstrate. They were so intense that I would often replicate the technique instantly after seeing the demonstration. There were no sports classes in my village but I heard that a good friend, Teodor, was planning to attend judo classes in the nearby town. I loved the idea but had no money, so he offered to let me join him for free. Why? Well, we had a plan.

One of my two best friends, Teodor was the son of the local priest. He lived just next door to me so although we were in different classes at school, we met and saw each other daily through the wire garden fence. As he was the son of the local priest, he would get most public things for free, including judo classes, so we agreed that I would be introduced as his brother (well, we looked slightly alike at the time) and would also get free admission. Although it was a couple of hours' walk, it was a good day out in the warmth of summer. We stopped for a swim at the lake that we passed on the way, and when we reached the first training class, I instantly fell in love with judo.

Shortly after, Ariel, the third member of our trio, joined us for training sessions. We all loved the experience and the fact that we were learning martial arts created a strong, healthy feeling about ourselves. A feeling of security and confidence united us and strengthened our character.

As the summer ended, Teodor stopped coming with us. Only Ariel and I made the trips to the judo training together, regardless of the snow, cold or rain, although we were only eleven years old at the time. Perhaps it was because of my strong desire and hunger to achieve, but after just a year my judo was as if I had been training for three years. I would fight guys that had been at the club for years.

"Vadim, you've got to enrol at LIRPS this year," said my judo coach, Phillip Batyr, accompanied by a typical waft of alcohol breath. "It is the best sports school in the country. Most of the Olympic participants are graduates of that school and you've got to be there. Only there can you grow further from where you are now. It is a tough entry exam but I'm sure if you prepare well you'll get in." This was one of the most amazing things I had heard. It could serve as a doorway on to the other side, where I could fulfil my hopes and desires.

Up until then, I had been hoping for the Pope to help me enrol into a theological school in Romania, or maybe an art school—I was constantly drawing pictures of saints or the local church by sitting on the roof of our house to get a good view. I thought that art or theology might have been my way out, but it was not clear when or how. But now, the opportunity to study judo at the best school in the country was just in front of me, and it made my heart beat quite happily.

Weird Remedy—Thoughts Create Reality and Build Character

My father was a sports fan, who always advocated eating well and exercise. He would wrestle and had built some DIY weights to lift, but it was all at the amateur level. Now, his son had an opportunity to get into a big professional sports arena and he was so happy, fully supporting me in my preparations for the enrolment and the exams.

The exams were in August and I had another two months to prepare, so I was out every morning running for about an hour. Then in the evening I was pulling myself up on the bars at our local school sports ground and occasionally would have another run. I thought all this would be sufficient for the exam, especially considering there was no one in the village doing anywhere near the same level of training.

About an hour and a half from the village, there was a concrete reservoir filled with water for irrigation. For the local children, we called this place "the pool", and we would gather there to play and swim among the frogs and snakes that dwelled in the same water. But one afternoon, I jumped unsuccessfully into the pool and my heels hit the concrete corner, splitting them open. It was not the blood and the pain that deeply upset me, but that I might miss my entry exam. If my father found out, he would get mad too, and this would get me into even more trouble!

However, I was used to getting my feet cut when swimming and playing in local lakes (a third of my summertime was spent in pools, such was my love of water and swimming) where unfortunately people would throw broken glass bottles and jars. The water was green or black so there was no way to see where you were stepping or landing. Anyway, I'd developed a therapy that worked like magic. Whenever I had a cut, I would put my bare feet on the road dust (there was no asphalt on the roads), which would cover the cut and stop the bleeding. I would keep repeating the procedure and by the time I got home late in the evening, my cut would be almost healed, with no pain. By the end of the next day, the cut was healed.

I had to reassure my father that the cuts would heal by the time of the exam and that they did not hurt, although it wasn't quite true. Despite the slight pain during the exam, I got through it but had to wait two weeks for the results. I was excited as I had made the first five in every exam before. I also trusted that my coach would have some influence, as he'd trained with the main coach from LIRPS in the old days.

Early Influence — Strong Mentor

I passed the entry exam and was enrolled at LIRPS. There I met one of the great influences of my life—my coach Vasile Luca. He had gone through the war and told us about the Nazi army, which he remembered well. I still remember hearing his memories of famine and how he and his family had to consume things like grass, or gather the sticky pith of sunflower stems to mix with wood shavings and then eat it like bread.

Mr Luca was one of the oldest coaches at LIRPS and a fascinating character as a person, coach and sportsman. He was a master in four different sporting disciplines: weightlifting, wrestling, judo and sambo (a kind of Russian wrestling quite like judo). He coached or trained with the majority of judo coaches in the country and was known by a lot of people. He had also trained generations of sportsmen. Year after year, the same surnames would reappear as parents who had trained under him brought in their children, knowing how he had changed their lives for the better. And most of the international judo medals won for the country were by guys influenced by him.

He was also the toughest and could kick your arse really hard if there was a good reason, which taught us all about character and attitude. He knew how to get the best out of you, and you would give more than you ever thought you had in you when he was at the training ground. He lived at the LIRPS judo base, although he had a place in the town where his son, daughter and wife lived. His kids were also at the school. We would see his wife once in a while visiting him there. He was a really fit and strong man and even at sixty-seven he won a national wrestling contest—against guys a lot younger.

Although he was known for his strictness and punishment-like assignments, there were numerous kids who were totally transformed under his influence from fragile children to real men of strong character. Vasile Luca remains a legend for his toughness and consistency. Many people give him credit for who they are—including me.

FIRST STEPS ON UK SOIL—DECISIONS THAT SHAPE CHARACTER AND BUILD THE FUTURE

Within my first few days of finally arriving in London, while my elder brother, Alex, was making calls to find me a job, I heard about a judo tournament and decided to visit it. I was so happy to meet my old friends from LIRPS Sergej and Arthur there. They mentioned that there could be a factory job for me but I would need to get an Italian passport, which would enable me to work. The passport didn't take long and soon after, I left my brother's home to go to Northampton where my friends lived.

That is where we started working at a factory manufacturing gym equipment. We had a common budget and bought a car so we could drive to work. But none of us could drive, so we had to decide who would be the driver. There would be no question of paperwork or a driving licence, as none of us had any genuine identity documents. We were nineteen and believed that we could do whatever we wanted. My father had a car and I had sat twice behind the steering wheel in my whole life—for a couple of ten-minute practices. Yet it was the best qualification between the three of us so we decided that I would be the driver.

We went driving through the town traffic, sweating profusely and often only in first gear! I was steering and moving the gears, Arthur was looking around and operating the indicators, while Sergej was watching behind and gripping the handbrake—in case we rolled back at the traffic lights or were heading wildly into a tree while looking for where to turn, as we had very little knowledge of the town. God knows how we managed not to kill ourselves or get arrested by the police for not possessing a driving licence or papers for the car.

As I had to repay the money my brother had borrowed for me, I started with my friends to work at two jobs: one for twelve hours, starting at 6 p.m. and finishing at 6 a.m., in a factory packing boxes with toys; and as we finished the night job we took a forty-five-minute journey to a building site where we worked for another nine hours. After finishing at the building site, we had another forty-five minutes to go back to the night job and thirty minutes to wash, which we did only a couple of times a week so we didn't waste time. Our work quickly deteriorated due to the sleep deprivation and tiredness. We were sleeping all over the place, but I was happy that I managed to pay off the debt.

After getting used to life and work in Northampton, I'd paid off my debts and was able to leave the crazy work shifts and rehabilitate. I had a good few days' rest before progressing to work in a much better factory, through two of my good friends. The Italian ID was not going to be accepted at the new factory so I managed to buy a proper passport—it is funny how products appear when the market requires it. When you lead a normal citizen's life, you don't see the things that can be seen the moment you enter into the shady world of illegal migrants.

I finally got the job and it was amazing. I was busy and being useful, and my friends were also there. Back home after work, we would drink some beer and have nice chats over a barbeque fire. What a beautiful life it was. Until one day, when we heard that our national insurance numbers .were going to be checked. At first, we had given the factory temporary numbers, reasoning that after the interview they would not bother about it, as there was no government check. This time they would be properly checked.

I decided to set an appointment with the Job Centre and try to get a proper insurance number. Everyone warned me against it, saying I would be arrested for fake documents, but I had heard that someone had succeeded with a passport very similar to mine. I decided to ignore the negative voices and go. That was how I first got arrested and ended up in prison.

Luckily, after three months, I was released on bail and I had to visit an office every week to sign in so they could keep me under supervision while deciding what to do with me. I had heard that some people did get papers and housing after a while of signing in, but then I got news of a guy who had been arrested and deported. I decided not to risk it and went to London, to rejoin my brother and some of my LIRPS school friends. I thought that it would be safer to get a new passport and start afresh.

I went back to London. I tried to work, but, since I believed that I could now just as easily be arrested for working as criminal activity, I soon realised that there were better and easier ways to make money. We had such a great team. We lived about ten in a house in east London, all judo or wrestling professionals. It was fun and I soon became the go-to guy for anything related to passports or driving licences. I had dozens of customers a day and made hundreds of fake papers. Soon after, I branched out into the "jeans fashion business" too, with a friend of mine Maria. She was a swift and smart girl who had learned a technique from a Romanian guy of making large thick pockets of multiple layers of foil to insert into a leather shoulder bag. This enabled us to put clothes with their security tags still attached inside the bag and avoid triggering the alarm while exiting the shop.

We bought an old Honda Civic and started driving to shopping centres around the country. As we didn't want to be remembered, we employed specific techniques: avoiding looking into the eyes of the staff while in the shop; visiting a store no more than once in two months; and taking only the most expensive stuff. In the evenings, we would then sell everything at half price, and could earn at least £200 a day. We would go to different towns around the country, selling the stolen merchandise to Moldovans, Romanians, Ukrainians and Russians. We travelled to almost every shopping centre in England.

Maria and I were a great team—we took the men and women sections and used a special routine to deceive the staff—however, eventually we were caught, at a shopping centre in Sheffield. I thought I would be sent back to prison. By then I had met the woman who is now my wife—Margarita. I had great plans for being with her, although she didn't know of them at the time, but I liked her so much that when they released us, I knew that I needed to drop criminal activity.

It was this same thought of getting myself out of the criminal world that months later led me to a Scottish airport and the prospect of making enough money in one go so I could quit.

It was a money fraud operation planned with a Nigerian gentleman I'd come across while looking for a way to earn more. The plan was to go to a specific currency exchange kiosk in a specific airport, show my passport and ask for a specific amount that would be waiting for me. The money was presumably hacked from someone's account and sent to another name as a simple money transfer. If I picked up those funds, they would be shared fifty-fifty between me and the "contractor". Each time the amount would be £3,000, and I planned to do a few of them while in Scotland. This was the first.

Why had I got into this? Well, this is where I felt the story of the pirate Henry Avery resonated with me, but I'll come to that. I was working at a factory for just £250 a week when I was asked to provide a national insurance number (NIN as per local work regulations) if I wanted to continue working there. It was the best work I had had so far and I wanted to keep it. Knowing my passport was fake, I decided to still give it a try—hoping it would pass.

I was arrested at the job centre and put in prison for three months.

After the three months, I was released on bail and had to report to the authorities every week, while I just waited to be deported once they had got all the paperwork ready.

Being sent back to my country, to my old life, at that time would have been like suicide (given my journey to arrive here and the debt I had to pay back), so I decided to move to London, disappear in the crowd and find something to do.

Now any encounter with the authorities or giving my fingerprints anywhere risked arrest again and being put back in prison—but for double time. Double time because I was illegal and also because I had not reported to the authorities since I had been released.

I started at a building site through a friend Michal, who found me a place working with him. But then there came an opportunity to earn more with fraudulent activities. It didn't take much for me to take the decision—the risk of being arrested at work and at the new activity was the same. I was illegal in both scenarios, so I went for the one that paid better.

This where the story of Henry Avery comes to mind. In The Republic of Pirates, Colin Woodard recounts how the first recorded pirate found himself and his ship stranded in Spain around 1694, abandoned by their country and at the king's disposal to "pay them or hang them if he pleased". Avery wandered the Corunna streets gathering up men from other English ships in the harbour in order to find a crew and a way to escape and return to their wives and children. First, they raided other ships to gather enough goods and a ship to get home. A few raids and some rich loot later, they realised that they could take advantage of the situation. The gang grew bigger, more powerful and hungry and turned to what we now know as piracy. This is how a person cornered with no option but to rebel transforms into a criminal or bites like a stray cornered dog fearing for its life!

Anyway, back to the story...

I was slowly approaching the small money exchange counter. On a piece of paper, I had the name of the sender, the amount of money and where I should collect it from. I was well aware that what I was doing was a complete fraud. I looked around for signs of the police or any sort of set-up that would threaten my safety, any hint of people and staff not going about their normal business or not moving around in a typical "airport manner". I had a troubling feeling just above my stomach—a slight warmth that felt like an alarm, a warning of love or danger. I was scanning my head for clues as to what was causing the feeling and it felt more like love than the other options.

It was almost a month from the moment Margarita told me she was pregnant, and in a few weeks, we would be going for a scan to see whether we were having a boy or a girl. I had started planning for something stable and safe to assure my child's future. I'd been involved in criminal activities for a while now and hated the risk and thoughts of guilt that came with it, but it seemed like the only option since I had no skills to make money any other way.

On the other hand, I had always had good grades in school and learned well, rarely from doing my homework but from absorbing the material just before the lesson began. My judo was still really good and I was always told that a good education and being successful in sport was the best mix a man could have. Why was I struggling to fit in? Had the world gone crazy or had I been deceived the whole time? Companies didn't want people with poor English and no experience, yet a smart and strong guy is the perfect fit for criminal activities.

These were my thoughts as I approached the little kiosk. I began double-checking that everything was safe: I just show the passport, take the money and off I go—piece of cake, right? I was so lucky to know people who gave me these types of "deals", but my gut feeling was telling me to run. I usually listen to those feelings as they are the only things I know that are right most of the time. Yet I couldn't walk away now—I was seven hours' drive from home and I needed the money. "I went to Scotland for a 'safe' deal and came back because I felt warmth above my stomach." Hmm, it didn't sound that smart, did it?

The precision of human perceptions are amazing. Business strategist and life coach, Tony Robbins was once talking about a great plastic surgeon who was visited by many celebrities. The surgeon said that the difference between ugly and beautiful is tiny, less than a millimetre—particularly the space between the nose and the top lip. Similarly, it only takes a tiny break in eye contact, say a millisecond, for your gut feeling to tell you a person is lying. We are very good at recognising these tiny details due to our highly evolved survival mechanisms.

I noticed that tiny eye movement and the almost invisible face muscle contraction as the cashier received my request and took my passport. Those little movements made my gut feeling become even stronger and more intense. Doubt increased but hope was still there.

"Just a minute, please," he said.

Time has some amazing properties. Although it is considered to be stable and measurable, every person perceives it differently according to the circumstances. The five minutes spent waiting for some important results compared with five minutes spent with a loved one are perceived completely different. This minute felt like hours. My whole life flashed before my eyes. *Shit, I don't like this*, I thought. I hoped the three police officers I saw were not coming for me. I needed to look cool and not show any signs of worry. Two more were coming from the other side... *Just stay cool.* If I ran, I would definitely not get the money. After all, these officers might just be walking around as they generally do in airports. It would be better for me to wait and pretend everything was fine.

Unlucky. They *were* coming for me.

The prison cell was a tedious, chilly place painted in a cold blue colour with a metal table attached to the floor, TV attached on the wall, metal bunk bed and a small loo. I was allowed out of the room for only two hours a day and another two hours while having meals and a shower. I had never felt so helpless and inhuman. The guy on the top bunk was from Iraq and spoke English even worse than I did. He would switch channels if the movie did not start with an explosion. From my bunk, I would try to catch a view outside through the two-inch gap of the metallic window frame, fitted with frosted glass. I would see just a pigeon and the Scottish sky, occasionally blue with the sun shining. And there was a high fence with barbed wire on top of it. My mind would then run through a theatre of memories, thoughts and ideas.

After three months with no books and just some paper to write or draw on, my prayers to the authorities were answered and I was permitted to go to the gym, take English lessons, pick up some books from the library and most importantly, attend plumbing and bricklaying classes, which I loved going to. These gave me real skills that I could use for my life outside, much better than my other knowledge, which had not got me anywhere, except prison. My English improved and my Scottish accent got even better! I became confident that when given my freedom, I would do something useful with all the new skills I'd acquired.

I was cut off from any contact with Margarita. I'd left her pregnant with no support or money and her visa about to expire, and it was torturing me. I was powerless. The pigeon I always saw by my window had the freedom. (However we think we are, sometimes all of us shed tears.)

That was the most excruciating moment of my experience there: being in the cell, walking it long and wide, crying at how stupid all this was. What will Margarita do now? Pregnant, visa coming to an end, and only £30 left to spend. She doesn't know how things work here, not even how to deposit cash in a bank account. How will she manage? Will she go home or be deported? Who knows when I will see her and my soon-to-be-born son? If I'm deported, how and when will I have a chance to meet them? This was a big and painful dilemma...

You see, I'd met her in London while she was there for a couple of months to study English. She became the love of my life and the mother of my beloved son, Alex. We could not spend an hour of our lives without seeing or at least contacting each other. Now we were separated for God knows how long.

The fact is that whatever the situation, you are in control. You can fix it. You can migrate from one situation to another—slowly and perhaps painfully, but it is possible. However, regardless of how hard I wanted to change things, I was behind thick walls. It seemed there was no chance even to try to change things when you were behind bars.

Eventually, the time came for me to be released and reunited with her. She'd been living with my friends from school. They had been a great help and amazing support for me and Margarita while I was inside. Now I had to move on, leave the criminal activities behind me and ensure that my family would be safe and looked after.

I started reading books, signed up for a website design course, bought a keyboard for £50 and started some piano lessons for brain development. A friend from my life of crime said to me, "What are you up to, Vadim, sitting here reading all these books and going to these seminars? Come with us to make real money and leave this bullshit. And what the fuck is it with these piano lessons? I think you need a doctor." Regardless, I persisted and soon attended a speed-reading course. It allowed me to consume books like biscuits. I was able to see so many ideas around me that could be monetised, and there was just not enough time in the day to carry them out.

One important part of your identity is your failures. Embrace them and learn from them. There is no one great person who never failed. Michael Jordan, who is considered the best basketball player of all time, said, "I've missed over nine thousand shots in my career. I've lost almost three hundred games. Twenty-six times I've been trusted to take the game-winning shot and missed. I've failed over and over and over again in my life. And that is why I succeed." He just made sure he tried again and again.

Consider identity as a brand—think of Nike, Apple, Gandhi—you build it, keep it and it will work for you and will earn you money.

To build a brand, either a personal or business one, you need a lot of physical energy, character and mental performance. I pay attention to the following:

1. Food—quantity, quality, timing—and water.

2. Exercise—take a walk instead of drive when possible, take the stairs when possible.

3. Character—prayer or meditation, express gratitude, write poems.

Further Reading: *How to Win Friends and Influence People,* Dale Carnegie; *The Rubaiyat of Omar Khayyam*; *The Prince,* Niccolo Machiavelli; *How Not to Die: Discover the Foods Scientifically Proven to Prevent and Reverse Disease,* Michael Greger.

3

GROWTH

Whether you believe you can do a thing or not, you are right.
Failure is only the opportunity to begin again more intelligently.
—Henry Ford

G ROWTH IS LIFE. You have to believe in it. Have
faith. Faith got me a long way. Without it, I would
have never get out of the country with only $200
in my pocket and no passport. I would never have left my
home and those things I was used and exchanged them all
for an unknown and almost impossible road.

You must be shapeless, formless, like water.
When you pour water in a cup, it becomes the cup.
When you pour water in a bottle, it becomes the bottle.
When you pour water in a teapot, it becomes the teapot.
Water can drip and it can crash. Become like water my friend.
—Bruce Lee

WHAT IS LIRPS? TAKING WHAT LIFE THROWS AT YOU AND DOING SOMETHING WITH IT

In 1996, I finally joined LIRPS and my dream of escaping from home to such a prestigious school had been fulfilled. Hooray! I was so happy to get this new opportunity and new challenge. And it felt great to have a change of environment, to live away from my parents and their alcohol-infused quarrels and fights that made me feel very uneasy. Although, it wasn't easy at first, only twelve years old and away from my parents. I could feel the amount of testosterone in the air and all these muscly, grim and scary-looking guys were a bit intimidating.

LIRPS was a sports-oriented school for students aged nine to eighteen. It was technically an orphanage school, though the number of actual orphans was quite small, and it was much more like a tough boarding school. The buildings interconnected by small concrete pathways, linking the classrooms to the canteen and a few wrestling and gymnastic spaces, including two for judo. There were also two small stadiums and one big one for football and athletics. Then there were three sleeping accommodation areas, which split up the students: one was for impact sports like judo, wrestling and boxing; one for other sports like chess, athletics and gymnastics; and the third was for girls. These were arranged in that way to avoid the impact sports bullying the less aggressive disciplines.

At about 6 a.m. the morning after I'd arrived, I was awoken by loud knocking next door, followed by an almost hysterical voice shouting, "Exercises!" When this was repeated outside our own room, it was so loud and scary that I rushed to open the door. But the loud-voiced old lady was already knocking on the next door and not paying any attention to me. The whole corridor was full of mostly newbies who had come outside just wearing their pants. We did not understand what was going on or what all the stress was about. We were just looking at each other thinking, "What is she shouting for?"

Three of us, me, Sergei and Anatoli, shared a single spartan room: three metal-framed beds, one large wardrobe and a table. We were all the same age and newly enrolled. Sergei was blonde and blue eyed. His father had also graduated from LIRPS and had had the same judo coach as his son. Those that had trained at the school would often send their sons and daughters back there, as they knew how important the discipline was and how good the place was for personal development. Almost always, the kid would be sent to the same coach as his parents were trained by. This would pass down through the generations.

Other things were passed down, too. Those graduating would always leave kit behind for those remaining. It was well known that given the lack of resources the new guys would not have much equipment to train with.

Generally, it was a nurturing culture with the strongest and most senior ones "educating" and taking care of the youngest. True, "educating" almost always meant kicking the young one's arse for his mistakes (or sometimes just for fun) or getting him to do chores or "help" wash clothing for the seniors.

My other roommate, Anatoli, though, didn't do chores for the seniors. His uncle had also graduated from LIRPS and he had good contacts. Anatoli was very confident and didn't fear those senior guys like I and the other newbies did. He would answer "Why me? I won't go," if told to go to the shop to buy something, or would refuse to hand over one of his own things when asked for it. Someone with no contacts or power would just have to do what he was told, otherwise his arse would be kicked. Those asking for "favours" would soon know who to back off from and go and find someone weaker they could pressurise. Those strong guys would also respect the good guys and they supported each other when needed.

Anatoli, Sergei and I were very close and friendly and looked out for one another when we were outside our room. My parents had only given me just enough money for a one-way ticket, and I had no money to go home for the weekend like many others did. I wasn't left alone though, and guys would often take me with them to their family homes where we had a great time and amazing home-made food. I loved it!

One day early in the morning, we heard an adult voice shouting, "Everyone get dressed and get outside!" I had seen the guy before helping the coaches and he seemed to know everyone. I learnt his name was Marcel. Marcel had a confident look in his eyes and the strength in his words were like those of a general commanding his soldiers. His tone worked—everyone moved and got dressed in a flash. It was the call for the 6:30 a.m. run.

My legs still hurt after the extreme run the day before. We ran continuously for two hours around the Rose Valley, a green park with three lakes. We then did twenty accelerating runs on a steep, thirty-five-degree hill. I thought I was dying and then the coach instructed us to do another ten frog jumps over a ten-metre distance. Some of the guys were vomiting and some just didn't want to continue. Someone whispered that "the Chief" (that I found out was our coach, Vasile Luca's, nickname, though it was only spoken between the students) would "open the season" with this killer training to filter out the lazy and the weak who would quit after the first day. (Never in my life had I had such heavy muscle pain—but I didn't quit.)

Marcel, as I've mentioned, has been a great influence on my life and even that day he had a look to his face—strong, but gracious, bright, kind and sincere—that made you trust him right away. I remembered I had seen him the first day I stepped into the school.

After we had finished the running and the Chief left one of the older students to instruct us. As we were waiting, we heard a shout. We turned to look just in time to see one of the senior guys smash another one in the face, throwing him to the ground almost unconscious. He then slowly walked back towards us. *What the hell is going on?* I thought. *What just happened and why? What will he do next?* At thirteen years old, I had only seen such an episode in movies. *Who are these people?* That fear of the unknown came back to me and I wondered if such violence would happen to me.

Sadly, I was right to be afraid. As we got back to the accommodation and were dressing to go to the canteen for breakfast, two of the seniors pushed their way into our room with about four of the other newbies who had been late like us that day.

"Everybody line up for *shoes!*"

One of the seniors ordered one of the new boys to lie on the bed face down, then, with a rubber large-size shoe in his hand, started slapping and smashing the youngster's bottom. We all looked at each other in fear and shock. The other senior, who was not slapping, started holding the poor guy down as he struggled to escape and ordered him to lie down again. We all unwillingly went through this process one after the other to learn that being late and not obeying the rules of the school was going to be tough.

My bottom was red, hot and hurting. I was scared and I wanted to go home! Some of the other new guys were crying. We were all young and feeling abused by these merciless older guys. I tried to calm myself down with the thought that at least I did not get smashed in the face like the guy did earlier—that looked so scary.

Afterwards, the three of us walked slowly towards the canteen discussing the earlier incidents. I was trying not to make any eye contact with any of those impudent faces of the seniors, who, I felt, were also discussing the morning incident but unlike us with smiles on their faces. I could not believe these things had happened—abuses I had never experienced or heard of before.

As we approached the canteen, there were about twenty people scrambling to form a sort of chaotic queue. The sun was shining brightly and the September breeze blew across the green landscape surrounding the narrow asphalt pathways to and from the school buildings. The air felt nice after the hot summer. We could hear loud talking, laughing and shouting among the hungry students, but it was not the normal buzz I used to hear at my old school, it sounded aggressive.

A sharp, strict female voice was trying to calm down the crowd: "Shut up, you crazy animals! Give him his bloody spoon!" We had to take our own spoon in to the canteen. And if one of the stronger boys forgot or lost his, he would just take one from one of the weaker boys, with or without his consent. The canteen lady I learned was "Aunty Elena", a former sambo champion and a very strict but equitable lady who was the only one whose requests (orders) most of the pupils would obey.

The other teachers were often intimidated or scared by the bullying students. These bullies were often criminals in the evening, robbing people of their clothes and stealing valuables. They were usually not afraid of the teachers because they knew that they would not be expelled due to their good sports performances.

As the newbies queued for food, we would often get a sneaky slap on the head from behind. When you turned around see who had done it, you'd see a group of seniors with a "haven't seen anything" look on their faces. Meanwhile, there would be another slap coming from the other direction, and as you turned round, there would be another slap from behind. Eventually you'd be covering your head with your hands as the slaps continued from all sides until you got out of the "queue". If anyone said who had been doing it, he would get a real slap in the face for being a "grass", which no one wanted as that reputation stayed with you forever.

This "queue slapping" happened in the main school building too, as you were walking to your classroom. It made me really angry and I soon got into a fight since I'd spotted the one who had slapped me. I was never slapped again after that.

Finally, we made it into the canteen to queue up at the collection window for our food. It seemed to me to be like a hospital or prison, the light blue and white painted walls and large, strong windows. I had heard that there was the kind of great balanced food here that a good sportsman needs. Well, there had been. The problem was in the past year the country had experienced an economic crisis and the quality of the meals had plummeted. Instead of the porridge with milk, butter and sugar in the morning, it was porridge made with water, no sugar, and only sometimes a cube of butter. It was followed by tea and a dried fruit compote. Those who were well supported by their parents brought with them a little paper cone of sugar. They were always attacked by a group of begging students.

In the evening, as in the afternoon, they gave us food made of pearl barley, which was rather tasteless, with no meat. This was a type of food that might have been prepared nicely at home, but was usually made poorly here. Today, the pupils were really unhappy with the food, which created a real mess. Someone switched off the lights and food started flying all over the dark canteen. The chaos continued for about ten minutes. After a number of attempts to control the room, even Aunty Elena had to hide under the coat rail by the entrance. I had never seen such a rebellion in my life.

The prospect of my first days of school classes had scared me to death before arriving. I have a stuttering problem (which I have worked on to improve, but even now still find it difficult when I have to introduce myself) and having to give my name was a nightmare—especially since my family name begins with 'T', which I stutter with more than anything else. I would sense the silent giggles, sometimes even from the teacher, which I hated. The more I got terrified by it, the heavier I stuttered, and this sucked. At least there were only four lessons in the day.

I was always glad to get back to the training, as I could perform and give my best, getting better and better every day. It balanced out the stress and embarrassment of the school learning time and my stuttering with words. The embarrassment I felt motivated me to press hard in sports and it worked out well. It was the only way I could succeed to get a bit of respect and compassion, to avoid being laughed at.

With my muscles still hurting from the Chief's killer session, I was called for my second judo fight, with a senior who had been at the school for three years. He was very strong and skilful but I was determined to succeed. He definitely didn't like that and made a sign that he would kick my arse after the training, for my persistence in trying to beat him.

I had another two fights during this training session and I could feel the steely look from the guy I had just upset. I tried to keep the fear away and to concentrate on my fights. By the end of the training, I had calmed down a bit and decided that there was no point in being afraid. Even if I were to get kicked around, he would not kill me. That felt good for some reason, and gave me a determined and confident look.

The senior had said he would be waiting for me after training but he wasn't there when I came outside. It was then I then learned that a good judoka will give respect to one that beats him and would try to win next time. This discipline and attitude is in all good sportspeople, so even if that guy had been there, others would not have allowed him to kick my arse without a good reason.

After dinner, we got back to our rooms and had some bread with water and a canned salad that we'd hidden under the bed—the canteen food was just not enough. I heard the older guys walking around asking for nice clothing for the night so they could go to the disco in the town. They would try to find someone from a better of family of an appropriate size who would have nicer clothing and perhaps even some aftershave. This meant everyone who would go to the disco smelling the same, but that was not an issue!

Later in the evening, we heard voices outside and guys jumping down from the windows. The accommodation was closed for the night and this was the only way to exit. We learned that one of our guys had been beaten up at the disco so everyone from every section and sport was gathering to go there and sort the problem out. Regardless how we were with each other in the daytime, everyone would join together to help anyone from the school when outside—a way of "protecting the school brand".

GETTING OUT—LET LIFE UNFOLD AND GO WITH IT

Many years after I'd first gone to LIRPS, I decided my current life was going nowhere and that I had to escape abroad. I planned to go with my friend Oleg but an unfortunate situation led to me going alone (more or less). Oleg and I were physically and psychologically ready and prepared to go through a "channel" (a migration route that avoided border checks) via Slovakia to Austria but my passport had been sent back with no visa for Slovakia because it was due to expire in the next three months and it needed to be six months minimum. We thought that Oleg could go by himself. At least Oleg would test the channel and give me the up-to-date details of the journey. He could also help me when I arrived there too. These thoughts cleared the negative feelings I had when I first got the passport returned.

It would take another three weeks to get the passport extended and a Slovakian visa. I hoped the authorities would not introduce extra measures within this period since we'd heard that Slovakia would "soon be a member of the EU". Meanwhile I began to learn some English words and sentences that would be of help on the way. I developed this technique that allowed me to memorise the numbers and letters very quickly. Whenever I was outside, I would spell and pronounce in English the number plates of whichever car I saw. I became very good at it.

It had been one day since Oleg departed and I was in waiting mode, hoping to hear from him. I had been envisaging what he would tell me after arriving in Vienna. *Perhaps he has already got a job and will be waiting to pick me up when I arrive?* I recognised this feeling from childhood: the expectation you feel on the morning of Christmas Eve. Impatient but happy! Almost one week later and no one had heard from him, he had not called his parents either and it did not feel good. Another two days passed by and Oleg then called from an Austrian prison where he had been detained, awaiting asylum. *He will be alright!* At least it meant that the channel was still open.

Adaptation — We Adapt and Grow Wherever We Are Placed by Circumstances

I am amazed by people—what they can go through and adapt to. On my journey towards the UK, having escaped from gangsters in Rome, I reached north Italy and was met by an old school friend of mine, Max. It was incredible how the migrant people lived there. Rarely would they pay for household goods—those things could be picked up from trains, toilets and other public places. Even with train tickets, Max had this technique to "fix" the ticket so it could be used an almost unlimited number of times.

While on the train, Max was telling me about his new life and how he had to convince his father to let me to stay at their flat for a couple of days. His father had to work hard—providing for his son and wife at home—and knew the price of what he possessed. I would be another person in the house that needed to be fed. I noted in my mind that I would have to be as unnoticeable as possible and help if and when anything was needed. Eventually it went from being a couple of days to three months, which concerned Max's father. A concern he would let be known after he had a little to drink.

My new passport was still in progress and my brother Alex was searching for sources to borrow money for my Brussels to London transfer, so there were not many options for me. I just tried to be of help and almost invisible. We were filling the fridge—by shoplifting from grocery stores—so there would always be enough food. We ended up having some lively times together. I learned to speak Italian while watching TV and speaking occasionally to people while asking directions and so on. It is a Romance language quite like Moldovan, so it was easy to learn. I was also a person inclined to learn languages so I had a real interest—it had been the same when I was in Slovakia and Austria earlier in my journey.

Soon after my reunion with Max, I thought we needed more clothes to wear. I was noticing all these clothes banks—large metal containers with a one-way door like the one for the cash at the bank, where you could only put something in and there was no way to take it out. These banks were located everywhere and we had the idea to break into some of them and update our wardrobe. But as we were assessing the banks and looking for ways to get into them, we realised that if we got caught, we would be punished exactly as if we had been caught shoplifting. Why not go directly into the shop and get some new clothes of the right size?

We became very good at that and soon had a nice wardrobe to wear. We got to know every shop and the way to get what we wanted out again. SO much so that sometimes we would walk in to see if there were any new releases. We were never caught but there was just one time when we were stopped. We had left one of the tags in the pocket and gone into another shop, but as it was not from their shop, it looked like an accident. We deliberately wore oversized clothing when we went into a shop, took a bunch of items we liked into the changing room and ripped the tag off. This left a small hole in the cloth, but it was not an issue for us as they were for personal use. However, we did eventually become a little more professional and stole a pair of pliers from one shop so we could take the tags off and not leave any holes.

I began to feel like a parasite. I was only taking and not giving anything back to the community, which felt slightly odd. I guess we were a product of our experiences and surrounding circumstances. I reasoned that if someone else had gone through the exact same experiences, circumstances and way of life we had led, they would be exactly the same. That it would work just like in cooking—you get the same dish with the same taste every time if you use the same recipe. Well, at least this theory worked for me, at the time.

WORDS ARE YOUR REMEDY

As I've mentioned, I grew up in a religious environment. As well as drawing saints and the local church, I read the Bible in three languages paying attention to the meaning in each one and comparing them. I also looked into the holy books of other religions. In every country I passed through, I would go to church at least once. I never minded what their religion was. I would just go and if I was asked my religion I would either not answered or lie—I didn't care about the name, I cared about the energy and tranquillity of the environment.

The Church had a big influence on me and I often relate things I read and see to the Bible. When it comes to the words we use, which I consider one of the most important parts of our development, I developed my own theory, related to my practical experience and the Bible.

The Bible says that in the beginning was the Word—that is where it all starts. Also it says that your sins will fall on your children and their children up to the seventh generation.

Well, I combined these two ideas. The words used in the home or by the parents imprint in the vocabulary of their children, then this gets passed on to their children, and so on. That is why the words that we use are so important and we need to pay attention to them and study them closely.

Your words can make you weak or make you strong.

Let me start with an example of weakening and empowering language:

Request:

"Hey, please help me do ..." or "Hey, join my ..."

Weak answer:

"Sorry, I **can't**, as I **have to** ..."

These words act on the subconscious level, making you weak and not in control of situation or not able to choose for yourself. At the same time, it shouts the same message in the subconscious mind of the listener.

Strong answer:

"Sorry, I am working on my project ... and will not ... this time. I definitely will ... consider it next time."

This puts you in a strong position, a position of being able to make a choice and decide what is the priority for you. People respect other people for their strong priorities, regardless of whether those are against their own desired outcome.

Less **can't**, more **won't**

Less **have to**, more **will**

Forming your question:

Weak:

> "**Sorry, can I ask** you…" or "I am really **sorry for bothering you**, could you please…"

Strong:

> "Hi, could you please do me a favour…" or "I think you are great, could I ask you…"

> This shows your determination and strong position and increases the chances of achieving the result desired. Instead of asking for permission to ask—as if what you're asking is unimportant—just ask as if what you want to ask is important.

> *The more you use these weak or strong wordings, the more you will realise people address you accordingly.*

Avoid categoricals—"always", "never"—especially in disputes or arguments. "You are always angry!" "You never say you love me!" Banish them from your vocabulary. Using them will put the person you are in a dispute with in a defensive mode and make them focus on the times when they did say, "I love you" or weren't angry, and so on, and they will begin trying to prove it instead of focusing on the resolution of the dispute.

Use:

> "You've been very angry lately" or "You are often angry,; and "Lately you very rarely say you love me," or "For a long while I haven't heard you say you love me."

These will keep the discussion on a realistic level and focus on the resolution instead of shifting on to how you are labelling the person.

Although I am not always perfect, I try to check my choice of words whenever I write a text or say something. I did this just now in a text message when someone asked me my opinion about a situation. I was just about to write, "I cannot advise you on this," but then changed it to a stronger version: "It's your choice, not mine." The thing is that I don't help anyone unless I am strong in my position.

Although this is an art in itself and there are many aspects to it, I wanted to give you some very simple examples here to raise your interest so you could start looking into it.

The measure of intelligence is the ability to change.
—Anonymous

Those who cannot change their minds
cannot change anything.
—George Bernard Shaw

Growth should be constant and every day. As you would not expect to have clean teeth for life after cleaning them well once, you should not expect to be ready for all of life's challenges after reading a single book or attending a seminar. You don't expect to have a great relationship forever after you give your loved one a bouquet of flowers for their birthday.

The best performers in this world, the ones that lead an amazing life, are constantly growing.

Educate yourself financially: what makes someone rich is how he manages money not how he earns it. The skill to manage money is more important than the skill to earn it.

What you are is what you eat, who you hang out with, what you read and what you say. So improve your diet, your network and your habits, plus, your physical exercise. Improve your skills and learn new ones: finance, leadership, listening, coding, sales, marketing.

For more inspiration, see what I am doing on my blog: vadimblog.com.

Multiple studies of the most successful people show that the following are the most common things they do, so why don't you start doing the same?

1. Create multiple streams of income

2. Save to invest

3. Surround yourself with high-achieving people

4. Be decisive

5. Be open-minded

6. Be persistent

7. Talk about ideas not things

8. Be comfortable taking calculated risks.

Further Reading: *The Selfish Gene*, Richard Dawkins; *Sleight of Mouth*, Robert Dilts; *Thank You for Arguing*, Jay Heinrichs; *Feel the Fear and Do It Anyway*, Susan Jeffers.

4

RELATIONSHIPS

PEOPLE ARE THE BIGGEST ASSET. Your network and the people you hang out with influence you greatly. There's a saying that you are the average of the five people you most spend your time with—so be aware of who you spend your time with. In sport, they say that in order to get better at your skill, you've got to have someone you can learn from, someone at your level you can practise with and someone you can teach your skills to. I think these are both great advice, but I'd add that you need to spend less time with, or ideally get away from, negative people and those who drain your energy or make you doubt your dream.

Be good to people and people will be good to you—even those who don't know you.

Become the friend you would want to have
or the person you would like to deal with
and bear the consequences of your actions.

My outlook and opportunities were narrow and the surrounding environment did not give many ideas, just poor opportunities, and so because I could draw well, I learned to forge passports when I first arrived in the UK. It was called *perekleyka*. The forging of passports was simple in those days and my artistic skills got me a long way. Soon those in need of papers for work or banking, as well as driving licenses and passports of all kinds came to me. There were two major suppliers of paper passports and plastic cards (IDs, driving licences, and so on) and they trusted only a few people with this work, of which I was one.

I would only supply people I knew well, around fifteen to twenty guys, or their friends, but this was still a massive market. The price increased with volume too, and there were huge margins on each document so the final buyer (who would use the false document) would be paying many times what I was paid. It was clearly at the top where the real money was being made, but it was hard for someone unknown like me to get there.

I learned the forging techniques from a man known as "the Artist". The Artist could forge any watermark, stamp or name on any document in such a way that no one would notice unless they had help from precision tools. However, most of the "forged" documents were badly done and since people would not know how they should really look or be able recognise a poor job they would get caught in banks or at work, and so on.

You do reap what you sow and for me that led to being imprisoned.

I wasn't caught for the fake passports, but the attempted fraud in that Scottish airport. So I ended up in a Scottish prison. Apart from the fact that my freedom was restricted and I was worrying about Margarita, who was pregnant, I was not doing so bad. I had great friends who sent funds to my account that I could use for the phone and weekly purchases. As I have said, I had been drawing since I was five. At school, this often helped me at school since I would be given money for judo or sports posters. This same skill helped me in prison too. Inmates would come to me with a picture of their wife and children and I would draw a portrait. This would earn me extra goods or food.

After five months, I was still not sure whether I would be released or deported. Margarita had come back from Russia and was now eight months pregnant, with her visa due to expire in about seven months. If I were deported, I would most probably not be able to come back to the country legally for many years and my wife would give birth to our child without me *and* with her visa about to expire. It was a messed-up situation I had got myself in. She was such a lovely, sweet, kind, easy-going and funny woman, we had shared so much together and it was eating me inside to not be with her.

I applied for any prison position in the hope of spending less time in the cell. I got a job cleaning the corridor after dinner, when everyone was back in their cell. The best position, though, was working in the kitchen as it gave access to food, so you could eat more or use it to exchange for products or favours. It was a highly regarded position and useful for those tough guys with connections. One of those was a tall, very fit and naughty guy, who I called "Gorilla". He would make fun of other inmates and told the most stupid jokes I ever heard—inappropriate in this environment, I thought. He would also pull down a guy's pants and get a big laugh out of it. Gorilla was usually accompanied by his cellmate minion.

I had been trying to call Margarita again but she had not been answering. When there was no queue for the phone, I tried again. Her mother answered and there was a long wait before Margarita came to the phone, nearly using up all my credit.

"Hi," she said.

"Hi, how are you? How do you feel?"

"A bit like shit, but it's OK," she replied. "I am a bit busy now, with my friends outside, let's talk later as I need to go."

"OK, I'll call another day."

And she hung up.

I hated that and wondered if her pregnancy was causing her mood swings. I wanted to smash the phone against the wall but held my anger back. I took the broom and started wiping the floor again, immersed in my thoughts.

I was very low profile most of the time and did not speak to anyone unless they spoke to me. I was just doing my time and avoiding getting involved in anything with anyone. My focus was on my studying and work so the time passed by quicker. No one, including Gorilla, would mess with me. And any fights and stabbings were mainly drug related.

I only had two mates there. One was the Lithuanian guy with whom I'd smoke roll-ups during the one-hour walk we were allowed. I would not have smoked otherwise but the conversation with him was refreshing and a change of routine.

The other guy I talked to was a kind person and a father of three girls—all from different mothers. Although I found him very kind and funny, very few of the other inmates would talk to him. I later realised this was because they were really intimidated by his cruel past.

One evening, while I was sweeping the floor, Gorilla pulled the stupid trick of pulling my pants down and my automatic reaction was to smash him with the broom in a quick impulse turn, without thinking of the consequences. He quickly threw two punches to my mouth that knocked me a step back but I swiftly replied with two jaw punches that put him on the floor. At that point, my hands were forced behind my back as both of us were dragged to our cells by two security guards. It was a fast intervention.

The next morning, Gorilla's minion visited my cell to mention that we would both appear in front of the prison governor and one or both of us, whoever was judged guilty of the misconduct, would be sent to into solitary confine-ment—not something that anyone would want.

I felt confident that it would not be me: I did not initi-ate the fight; I was half his size; and in any case surely the whole thing could be checked on the CCTV? Still, I had to be strong and not show any weakness so I summoned the minion and told him, in an authoritative voice, to inform Gorilla that I had an idea of how we could both come out of it alright with the governor.

The next morning, I met Gorilla in the waiting room by the governor's office, and, following our prepared story, I smiled and said hello. He smiled back and saluted. His jaw was inflamed with lumps on both sides, which looked rather painful.

"So what happened?" the governor asked me first.

"We were just playing a boxing game, sir."

We both were let off and from that day Gorilla would always give me extra food as he still had the best kitchen job. His attitude improved too.

KEEPING THE BLOOD TIES—IT IS FOR LIFE

After my torturous journey through Europe, when I finally reached the UK, I was so looking forward to seeing my elder brother. I hadn't seen Alex since he had arrived in the UK and we had only been communicating irregularly by phone. He had now an Estonian passport, new name, and was working at a building site. He had quickly moved from being a simple labourer to a "master" and a higher salary.

Though Alex and I had got along really well when we were young, I hadn't seen him much since I had gone to LIRPS when I was twelve. He is four years older than me, and before I went away to school he would often take me with him to various gatherings, movies and even discos. He joined the army when he was eighteen and we then mainly wrote letters to each other. He would draw some pictures and I would send him some judo drawings too. I missed him a lot when he went to the army. I liked to share with him my sport performances and I remember writing to him about my all wins when I was doing well in my first year at LIRPS.

Soon after returning from the army, he found there was not much to do in Moldova and he went to Moscow to work. He'd been there for a couple of years when an opportunity opened for me to help someone to go to the UK, so I decided to arrange for Alex to also go as he would have a better life there.

YOU ATTRACT WHAT YOU ARE AND BECOME WHAT YOU THINK ABOUT

I have seen angels in people. I had reached Austria with a new friend, Slavik, and we were hiding in the Vienna Woods but had run out of money and food and we were almost starving. Finally, I managed to make contact with a fellow Moldovan. He sent his girlfriend to meet us and bring us to their flat.

We had never met them before in our lives and we were so dirty, smelly and tired when we arrived at their apartment. There were about four guys living in the apartment and two girls who were the girlfriends of two of the guys. All of them were living in a one-bedroom flat. In the bedroom, there were two beds and a mattress and in the living room was a sofa bed. It was rather cramped. We were there only for one night and the plan was for them to show us to the train that would take us to Italy. Slavik had an uncle there and he might be able find some work and accommodation for us.

Even though we were going towards Italy, all the time I had the UK in my head as my final destination. But I'd decided I would try to play along and adapt to whatever life threw at me while I was heading there. I had been to a number of countries during my sports career including a few times to the UK—where a few of my sports pals had remained after not returning home from a tournament. They were established there and had good jobs and so when I compared their life and occupations with those of the people I had met on my journey so far, I was definitely drawn in the direction of the UK.

When we arrived at the apartment in Vienna, one of the girls told us about how they got into the country and what we should do if we got caught by the authorities. She told us the German word for asylum, *asyl*, since if we were caught we needed to ask for it. If we told some terrible story, they would not send us home but hold us there and that would give us a chance to get legal papers. Technically, it seemed we were safe from the threat of deportation back to Slovakia or Moldova.

We had the alarm set for 6 a.m. so we could be at the train station to get the 8 a.m. train to Italy to Slavik's uncle in Verona. Just before the alarm went off, we were awoken by a loud knock on the door. It was a police raid. I told myself that whatever the cost I would not go home or be deported back. We panicked and I ran to the window ready to jump out from the third floor and Slavik hid in the wardrobe. But I eventually held back as I had been reassured that if I told a good story I would not be deported.

We were driven to the police station where we asked for *asyl*. We were both placed in a cell and given some food. In the room there was a metal bunk bed and a metal table and chairs. Nothing was moveable and nothing had sharp edges—everything was extra safe.

We had been told a story by one of the guys from the flat about someone who was released from prison after stealing from cars. He was about to be deported but he went on hunger strike. He did not eat for about two weeks or so and avoided deportation. That story was in our head and we decided not to eat. We obviously had no idea why and for how long we would be there but we knew that we needed to use all known means to avoid deportation.

I am still grateful to those guys and their girlfriends that followed us to the police station explaining what we should tell the police and translating for us what the police officers were saying. They were a great help. They had taken us from starving in the woodlands and given us a chance. They told us how many people like us they had assisted but also that nobody got back to thank them after leaving. I am sure those others were, like me, very grateful but too busy with their lives or lost in time to make contact and thank them. However, I am sure karma will do what's right.

I consider myself a very lucky person given how much help I got from random people. Perhaps it's because I too lend a hand when I see someone in need.

Things happen when people care.
"Ask and it will be given to you; seek and you will find;
knock and the door will be opened to you." Matthew 7:7

After three months of being in a waiting and surviving mode in north Italy, I received good news from my brother, Alex. He had found the money to pay for my Brussels to London transfer. It was my time to leave Max, and I planned to take the next available opportunity. It was important to plan to avoid any passport checkpoints for this trip. I had got some information that if you were travelling by train through the night and fell asleep, the conductor would politely avoid waking you up to ask for your passport. That seemed the best solution. My idea was to get the next available evening train to Brussels, changing trains in Paris. The train set off from Milan at around eight in the evening and so would reach the French checkpoint at night, which would be a great time to be asleep.

That evening on the platform, Max and I wished each other well and exchanged big hugs and then I stepped aboard. It was again time to ask God to help me through the challenge—it had worked for the previous challenges. I walked into my compartment. There were three bunk-style couchette beds on either side. On the bottom, two beds slept two Asian-looking guys. They were clearly immigrants—I had encountered many of them before and could easily spot them from afar by now. It struck me that these guys were doing exactly what I was planning to do—crossing the border north without legal papers.

The compartment had this sharp, long-unwashed-socks smell, which was terribly unpleasant. As I looked around to choose my bed, I heard the conductor right behind me. He had walked in before I had a chance to "fall asleep", which was very unfortunate timing. He eyed the sleeping guys and proceeded to ask me for my ticket and passport. While I was searching to get the ticket out of my bag, he sniffed and got a special key out and opened the larger window so the smell could go away. (The usual small window that was already open could not cope with the job.)

I pretended I hadn't heard about the passport and handed him my ticket. He repeated the passport question. I began fishing for the "passport" in my bag and then pockets, while contemplating which would be the better option: staying and just running off the train now. Eventually I said that I'd forgotten my passport and he asked me to follow him to his compartment. I was begging him to let me travel and that it was very important for me to get to Brussels. When we reached his compartment, he asked how much money I had. All I had left was fifty euros, which was hidden in an internal pocket of my shorts. His face showed that he did not believe it and also that he was not happy with the amount. I emptied all my pockets and took everything out of my backpack to show that was all I had and he eventually succumbed to my begging.

He told me that above the top bed in our compartment there was a luggage shelf. He ordered me to lie on the luggage shelf and not move from there for the whole journey, not even to go to the toilet, until we reached Paris in the morning. When we reached there, he would come and take the money from me, as he would have been checked before that and would not have been allowed to have extra money on him. It sounded like a plan, although I would only understand later why he wanted me to lie on the luggage shelf instead of in my bed.

When I got back to the cabin, I saw that my theory about the other guys was correct. They immediately asked me why I was taken away, if I had a passport and what the conductor had said to me. They had recognised me as being one of them too. After I'd spoken to them, I went to the toilet to make sure I didn't have to go for the duration, jumped up into my new "lounge" and shortly fell asleep.

I was awoken by loud chatter in the compartment, but as the conductor had instructed, I did not move. It was the border police and they were talking with the two Asian guys. Eventually the police took them away. I was now the lucky one, I thought. If my initial plan had gone as intended, I would have not encountered the conductor and might have been taken by the border guards too. It was a lucky escape.

I continued to lie motionless. It was already morning and at the next stop some new people came into the cabin. They were French, two women and a child. They got out some snacks and drinks and were having a chat, not noticing me at all. My head was spinning as I contemplated different scenarios, such as what would happen if I had to give my last money to the conductor? Would I even be able to get from the Gare de Lyon station in Paris, where I'd arrive, to the Gare du Nord to get the train that would take me to Brussels? I would be stuck in Paris with no options and no money. These thoughts were torturing me. Even to find someone to help me in Paris would take calls that I could not afford.

An idea struck me: if I managed to get off this train, I could take another train to Brussels. I knew I could not get out of the cabin as it was against the conductor's advice and who knows what he would do if he saw me trying to escape—I could not take any risks. The large window was still open after the conductor had opened it to get the smell out. I could fit through it! This was the best low-risk plan and I thanked God again that he'd turned another problem into an opportunity.

It wasn't quite as low risk as I'd thought (as you'll hear in Chapter 7 "Timing"), but I finally arrived in Brussels with just my a few euros in my pocket. I was walking around the station in search for a coin-operated phone so that I could call people to pick me up. All of the machines were card operated so I had to buy a card in order to call. The problem was the cheapest card was €5 and I only had €3.40 left after purchasing a new ticket to Brussels. I went card hunting and I wasn't shy about approaching people for a card. I knew that I would not mind giving a card to someone with a few euros on it myself.

The strategy was to spot someone that was already on a call, wait until they finished and ask for the card if there was any credit left, while offering my €3.40 in return. It worked! A young lady kindly offered me her almost full €5 card and would not accept my money. People are just amazing.

Communication and character play a big role when it comes to the most important skills, especially entrepreneurship and business—in other words, working with people. Being able to work in teams, delegate and lead are crucial in building something big.

A substantial addition to your leadership and people skills is the ability to listen. Here is a story: A young boy was the son of a tribal chief and often went with his father to tribal meetings. He remembered two things from those meetings: first, they always sat in a circle; and second, his father was always last to speak.

That is how Nelson Mandela answered the question of how he learnt to become one of the greatest leaders in the world.

Keep your opinion to yourself until everyone has spoken. This skill gives everyone the feeling they have been heard and they have contributed, and also, it gives you the opportunity to hear everyone's thoughts.

Further Reading: *Nonviolent Communication*, Marshall B. Rosenberg; *The Power of Your Subconscious Mind*, Joseph Murphy; *Winning Arguments*, Jay Heinrichs; *Thinking, Fast and Slow*, Daniel Kahneman.

5

ASPIRATIONS

If you're gonna make a change, you're gonna have to operate from a new belief that says life happens not to me but for me.
—Tony Robbins

ALWAYS HAVE A GOAL IN MIND or a dream. Never let the goal pass by without it being achieved—see it, smell it, taste it, feel it whenever you close your eyes. If you don't have one, make one—however ridiculous or unreachable you think it is.

Ask people for help. Never go around town looking for a petrol station without asking for the directions from someone.

Read stories and biographies of people that have already achieved what you want to achieve—there is always someone who has done it or done something similar. Find those people, find their events and attend them.

Do the best you can and be patient—when you do things right with all your heart, right things will come to you.

FEEL THE FEAR AND DO IT ANYWAY

Aged nineteen in the spring of 2004, I was deeply disappointed by how uncomfortable and disadvantaged my life seemed to be after I had achieved results in judo I could only have dreamt of five years earlier. The disappointment affected my attitude and my focus on training—as a result, my winning gold medals was diminishing at a fast rate. I was giving up and my thoughts turned to making a change: to escape abroad. I needed to find a step-by-step guide on how to cross the border. My options were scarce—I could not afford to pay to an organisation to get me to the other side. The only available route was to "walk".

"Walking" meant finding a way to get close to a border and to cross it somehow by actually walking over to the other side in an area with few border checks, or hiding in a car, or swimming or taking a boat across a river. If someone were to get across successfully, it would create a route known as a "channel". These channels would often change, since as each new one was discovered, it would quickly be uncovered by the authorities because of the volume of people flooding through. Usually a channel would be usable for six to eighteen months.

A friend of mine with many connections among the "walkers" set up a meeting with one of his friends to give me information on a relatively fresh channel that I could use. This had to be more reliable than relying on rumours. It was a meeting with someone who had actually done it and I felt blessed for the given opportunity.

As he gave me instructions, I took notes. "You first get a visa to Slovakia—it's quite easy and cheap to do that now. I've heard they will be joining the EU in the next eight to twelve months, so you have some time. Slovakia borders Austria and that is your way in." He continued giving me all the other details: how to take a van to Bratislava, then head to a large building with a Coca-Cola sign, pass under a footbridge over a green field, cross a river and then finally climb aboard a wagon of an industrial train full of logs, scrap metal and paper, and hide in it. That would take me to Austria. It was high risk—other guys had suffered broken legs, suffocation and some had even died.

He gave me so much detail including how to check for the right numbering on the wagons—for a good reason, if I got on the wrong train I'd be heading east to somewhere in Belarus! Usually the trains would come and go regularly, but some would wait there for days, so if you hid and the train did not move within the hour, you had to get off and find another. When the train arrived at the Austrian border it would be thoroughly checked for about forty minutes so it was important to get an evening train in order to be less visible.

After the border check had been completed and the train had pulled away, it would be safe to come out of hiding. After forty minutes, the train would enter a warehouse and that would be Vienna. The idea was to jump off as the train slowed down *before* it reached the warehouse. However, because of the proximity to Slovakia the border police were active and reacted very quickly to any high level of migrant activity. At the same time, the local people also reported all suspicious people. So a change of clothes would be needed to look cleaner and less obvious.

Further instructions were to jump off the train on the left side towards the fence by the motorway, which would lead to a Vienna suburb and decide on the direction from there. I could wait by the woodland for someone to pick me up, but not too long because the locals would notice and report me. My other options were then to either head towards Italy on foot, or to steal a car from somewhere in the neighbourhood. Or to go into town and ask for asylum from the authorities, but it had to be in the town or I would just be immediately deported. The advice was to take little extra clothing and just Snickers bars and oat biscuits to eat, as both were a good source of energy.

DITCH THE UNSATISFIABLE REALITY

The last competition I had participated in was a failure. My body and mind had been filled with the forthcoming trip and the possible opportunity. I was defeated by a fighter that I would normally have beaten. This also contributed to my decision towards the departure from the country.

I heard my conscience tell me: "There is nothing else here waiting for you, your shoes have cracks in them and you look like shit in these old second-hand clothes. Look at your results, today you lost, your club doesn't need you any more for tournaments abroad, and they will just take the other guy who beat you, even though you are the strongest in the category! You need to go and never to come back.

There is nothing here for you, and you are capable of doing much more in the land of opportunity."

Despite my decision and determination to carry it through, the fear of change was not leaving me either and had something to say: "You need to concentrate on your judo! You are very good and have a chance for the World Championships and even the Olympics if you train hard enough. If you win, there are financial rewards for you and you might even qualify for an apartment, like some of those judo guys you know. You can do even better, you just need to concentrate and train hard enough. Don't go there, no one is waiting for you. You don't know the language and you don't have a proper opportunity like you have here. It is stupid to exchange something you have for just hope, which doesn't have any real value. What if you get caught and put in prison? You will then lose the only asset you currently have—your judo skills. Or imagine you get injured or even something worse—all of those risks exchanged just for hope? You are fucking stupid!"

I was feeling very confused and I didn't know what do to. Despite my poor performance, it wasn't an important competition and the management would probably not pay too much attention. I would just win the next national tournament to prove my position. But what if this did not happen? My only shoes had holes in them and I could not afford a good quality new pair. I did not like buying cheap clothes. A couplet by Omar Khayyam came to mind: "You had better starve than eat whatever, and better be alone than with whoever." I decided to toss a coin, as I normally did in this type of decision-making situation when two of the choices had the same strength. Heads, I go, tails, I stay... Heads!

Oleg was one of those friends I considered as a brother and whom I could trust and share everything with. When you have known someone from a young age at school, you get to see them in all kinds of surroundings and different life situations, especially those that are really hard. We were strong as long as we were united in any circumstance, and that made us more like brothers. We had grown up together and we had so many common interests. When I outlined the plan to him, he liked the idea and decided to join me on the journey.

Our first step was to make up a credible reason to get our passports from the management. Our passports were always with our manager as he was the one organising all the visas for overseas tournaments and the plans for training. There were no other times we would need the passport and that was why it stayed with the management. I came up with the story that we were going with my parents to the seaside, and luckily we had no tournaments planned for the next few months, so they agreed to let us have our passports. We gave our passports to a tour agency and then had a two-week wait for our visas. During that time, we were daily looking at the Europe section of the atlas, envisaging our travel plans.

As I have already related, my visa was delayed, so Oleg went by himself. The channel worked, but he was caught and seeking asylum in Austria. A week before I was about to set off by myself, one of the former LIRPS judo coaches (a guy in his late thirties) decided he wanted to come with me on the trip with two of his friends, one in his early forties and the other in his early twenties.

Our best choice for the spare clothing to go on this "walk" was some sports gear that we had been recently given by a company as a kind of charity help. The gear was in a silk-like material of a salad green colour from at least four seasons back. It scored zero for fashion but ten out of ten for practicality. A friend called Igor kindly "lent" us his good quality backpack. It had an extra strap that clicked shut at the chest, which allowed it to stay firm on your back when you were running. He didn't know of our real plan and that we would not be able to return it.

In the backpack, I put the clean change of clothes and the food reserves. As I had no idea if I would ever be back in my country I decided it would be best to visit my parents beforehand. I often avoided visiting home due to their alcohol problem, and would mainly visit them in the school summer holidays, if I was not preparing for a tournament, and some occasional short trips.

After two days and one night with my parents, having long conversations and remembering the past, my mother walked with me to the gate for our usual goodbye hug and kiss. They would have both walked with me to the bus station if they had known that this was the last time they would see me for the next ten years. I knew she kept secrets well, even from my dad, and I had a desire to tell her what I was about to do. But this time was different: they might try to stop me or worry too much about me if they knew what I was planning (and how I was going to do it).

On the day of departure, I had mixed feelings. I arrived twenty minutes earlier than our agreed meeting time at the Hotel Inturist in Chisinau and waited for the other guys to arrive. I felt almost normal, just mildly excited about the trip. We headed off quickly and after ten hours of driving we arrived in Bratislava.

BURN THE BRIDGE

It is easier to reach your goal after you've made the first step.

Bratislava was the last stop on the first leg. Dusk had not yet come and we easily found the building with the Coca-Cola sign and then the footbridge that had been described to us. My initial plan was to go right to the river and get on to a wagon or at least be waiting for the appropriate train in order to arrive at my destination as soon as possible. Every hour wasted was burning inside me.

Instead, we ended up taking a room together in a motel minutes away from the "target location" because we had found out that the train we were supposed to jump on to would be leaving the next day. There were a dozen young people with the same plan as us, waiting to cross in the same way. A lot of them had been here for weeks, and some even longer—up to three months. They were sleeping in a nearby park and eating all sorts of rubbish while waiting for the right time, for the right train with the desired cargo. Every evening, they would come to the "spot" and wait for the train. They learned the schedules of the trains and had seen a lot of drama—we heard stories of people getting hurt and guys that were electrocuted to death. They also told us about all the people that had tried again and again in vain. I tried not to pay any attention to the stories. I was there to follow those people that had crossed *successfully*, just like Oleg who had got through first time.

Those stories negatively influenced the guys I was with though. The two older ones decided not to risk their lives and families (quite rightly, perhaps) and dropped out. They were not in my position where I had burned all my bridges, and they had a different lifestyle back home from me. Their motivation level was not as high as mine, and it was shattered by the horror stories they had just heard.

The younger guy was also affected by the stories and did not want to go ahead, but the other two more mature guys persuaded him to go with me in the evening. As this was also a border area, you had to be careful and move cautiously to avoid being visible. We crawled through a grass field heads down as a searchlight swept over it. Then we approached the river. Its banks were lined with bushes and tall grass, which was a useful hiding spot while waiting for the train, and the whole place was heaving with people. Although you could not see anyone, you could feel and hear the human presence, whispering and breathing. You could hear a lot of Russian, Ukrainian and Moldovan in the air.

The "right" train did not arrive that evening. We learned that the train that did pass was full of tree logs. It would have been extremely dangerous to jump on while it was moving and you'd have almost certainly been crushed by a huge wooden log. I was still full of energy that night and took the experience as a warm-up before the challenge. If I had not been assured by the "professionals" that the train coming the following day would be safer, I am sure I would have jumped on to the log train. I was surprised how well informed those guys were, although there was no action. They were just waiting for something safe to hide in. But I knew the safe cargo would be checked more thoroughly, so "comfort" was not my goal.

KEEP YOUR EYES ON THE GOAL AND WALK THROUGH

Finally, I got the "right" train with some other guys (the younger man I'd come with eventually bailed out) and after a very uncomfortable ride, we arrived in Austria and jumped out of the dirty and cold, scrap metal-filled wagon into the woodland belt I had been told about. The area, which was part of the famous Vienna Woods, looked like a crash pad! There was a bunch of thin branches that had obviously served as a bed. There were clothes lying here and there, which I presumed were dirty from stowing away in goods trains and had been left there by travellers like us. And food packaging and other rubbish was scattered around. This was obviously a well-trodden route. The energy rush subsided, and we realised we were all tired and needed a good sleep. We also gathered some branches into rectangular shapes to form beds and lay down.

It was late April of 2004 and the nights were rather cold. I was woken up by a sharp, chilly, painful wind whistling in my ear and going into my brain. I looked around and found a discarded pullover and a razor. I used the razor to cut one of the sleeves off and then put it on my head to cover my ears. By early morning, all of us were awake, prompted by the feeling of hunger, and we began walking through the woodland in search of food. Two of the guys found some small spotty eggs, which they quickly ate.

We found other nests and purpose-built large bird feeders and installations for birds to drink water from. I noticed how beautiful the surrounding nature was. The smell of freshly cut grass in the air reminded me of my homeland. The rabbits jumping in the distance and deer walking looked like the movies and cartoons I used to watch as a kid. You could not see those animals in my home country unless you were hunting, which I never did. This had a feeling of a calm and peaceful place, where the nature was cared for and looked after. The grass was nicely cut and the bushes were nicely shaped with everything as if it were part of a nice artistic picture. The trees, the bushes, the grass, animals and houses that you could see from a distance just looked to be in the right place, like they were made for each other as part of a great design.

In the full morning, everything looked different, though. We were in a fairly small patch of woodland and there appeared to be houses surrounding us in the distance. Objectively, it was hard to see how we could walk and reach any sort of real countryside—we would either get caught or it would take us months. I had to find someone to help us. I took out my little Filofax. (It's funny how they looked. They used to be a brilliant idea but disappeared after the mobile phone became popular.) I loved it for its practicality, only 6 cm by 3 cm. I'd noted down the names and phone numbers of friends, and friends of friends, who might be of use on my journey. One such person was a guy in Rome who could give me $100 that he owed to Vitalic, a good friend of mine. I did eventually go there to pick up the money, which ended up being an unexpected twist in the story.

I decided I would go out, find a phone and make a few calls to find someone that could come and pick us up from this place. We all looked like chimney cleaners, with our faces and clothes all covered in rust from the train. Unfortunately, none of the other guys had spare clothes so they just shook theirs to get some of the dirt out. I was the only one with spare clothing, which I changed into. There was no water anywhere, so I went to the bird drinking place and washed my face in that water to look decent and clean before going out to look for a phone or whatever I could find to help us get to out of there.

The salad-green outfit came in really handy. As I headed out to make some calls, I walked and started stretching and then started jogging and punching the air like a boxer to act like a proper sportsman. I estimated I'd reach the town in about thirty minutes. A cold shiver passed through my body with every car that drove by. Especially as there were not many of them and it felt as if it was only me and the car in the whole area. I felt unprotected and threatened by the chance that I could be reported.

A woman came jogging towards me and I waved at her as she passed me by. I noticed that she waved back, so I waved at the next two joggers I encountered and they also waved back. It was working and it was a relief. From then on, whenever I went out to make a phone call, I would put on the same act. Finally, I found a phone box about a one-hour run from our "home". I got some change from a local shop and started calling the numbers I had in my book.

After two days and about five trips to the phone box, I still could not find anyone to come and pick us up. I would spend almost half the day in town trying to call people. If the number did not answer, I would try again a few hours later or the next day if still unavailable. Some of those that picked up did not have any idea where we were, as Vienna is a large city and there are many train stations with woodland nearby. My geographic explanations did not help locate us very precisely. I had too little information about the local town so I described it visually, which I suppose made it sound very similar to many other Austrian villages or towns.

Not only would the place be hard to find, but it must have been hard to decide to go and pick up five people you didn't know, with no idea what would happen next. People were also busy with their own lives. None of the guys I had crossed with had money, and my €200 was slowly being used up with the calls. I did not buy more food to allow the budget to stretch as far as possible, as I didn't know how long we would be there. Nor did any of the guys have any food and we had to extend my Snickers bars and oat biscuits as far as we could.

With every trip, I felt more and more exhausted from hunger and thirst and would sometimes drink water from a puddle. My jogs were less and less energetic and I was feeling small spasms in my muscles from the lack of nutrition. We decided that we needed to make a move, as hopes of being picked up by someone were diminishing with every unsuccessful phone trip. Staying there any longer would only have led to starvation.

Up to this point, we had all hoped that my plan would succeed and we would be picked up. When that didn't happen the unity and team spirit went and I could feel in the air that everyone was already contemplating their own ideas. Not that it bothered me. I had bonded with one of the guys, Slavik, and he knew a friend of a friend living and working in Austria, and he was sure this guy would know where we were and how to find us. Meanwhile, the other three decided to go into town, break into a car and set off. We parted and I gave them €40 out of my remaining €160 to buy food. My supply of Snicker bars and biscuits had finished earlier in the day.

Slavik and I were left in the woodland. Hearing voices in a nearby field, we came out of the trees and looked down from the top of the hill and saw some young guys having a late picnic. We knew they would leave behind some food for us to feast on and perhaps some bottles of drink. With the level of energy we had, this was an ideal solution. We waited for hours, which felt even longer.

We had lots of time to discuss where we were from and our previous lives. And we imagined what it would be like to run at those picnic people like hungry wolves to eat and drink whatever they were having.

We were amazed by the civilised manner of those youngsters. They had a long picnic, eating and drinking for hours until late at night, but did not leave a single thing behind, not even a tissue—the place didn't look any different than before they came! Surely this was a different kind of breed of youngsters from those we were used to—very well educated and raised by their school and parents. We ended up sucking the sap from grass blades again before going to sleep.

We were into our fourth day in the woods and were becoming hysterical. In the morning, I went to the phone box again. It would have to be the last time. It was also the hardest one as I was so weak and exhausted that I could not do any of my sporty moves and I'd become more concerned about survival than being caught. I greeted Slavik's contact on the other end of the phone and explained who I was, who I was calling on behalf of and asked if he could pick us up. He knew exactly where we were, how to get to the nearest train station and where we needed to hop off, so we could be met by his girlfriend on the way back from work. We would need to wait until about 7pm on a particular platform so she could meet us.

It would take thirty minutes to get to the station where we agreed to meet the girlfriend. We left two hours beforehand just in case anything happened on the way. We followed all our instructions and hopped on to the train. It was weird noticing through the train window, our three friends forcing their way into a car that was parked on the road. My English, which I had been practising before leaving Moldova, came in really handy when purchasing the ticket and asking how to get to the particular train station and the platform number to wait on. The girlfriend was there to greet us. She knew who we were but just to make sure she asked who we were waiting for and then we boarded the bus towards their flat.

Steps Before the Mission Is Completed

When I had finally reached the UK, I found my elder brother, Alex, had got an Estonian passport and was working at a building site. Some time after he was arrested and put in a detention centre to be deported. I was greatly upset. Although I had my friends, I loved him and he was the only relative of mine in Britain. I also knew that he had not saved much money to live with if he was deported and my heart was bleeding.

One day, I received a letter from him telling me of his plan to escape. He was going to jump off the roof of the detention centre and climb over two fences. He wanted me to be waiting for him in a car, ready to speed off.

We agreed on the plan, where to wait, and a code language to use.

The day of the escape came and I set off with my friend Victor. We had some slight fear but were determined to carry out the plan. We did not think about the risk to us. We were just hoping that Alex would succeed. We arrived at the meeting place just before darkness fell, with the car lights off. We were ready for a quick exit and got out to search for Alex. By now all kinds of thoughts were going through my mind: "If he is caught, what they will do to him? What if he had an accident while climbing and jumping over those tall wire fences?" Suddenly, I heard a noise and quick movements about a hundred metres away. I headed slowly in their direction. There was a violent shake and crack of branches in some bushes. I whispered loudly, "Alex! It's you?" I could not believe the happiness and the weirdness of the situation. We had a great hug, quickly got into the car and drove with our lights off until we got to the main road. Until halfway back to our home in Ilford, east London, we could not believe what was happening and were looking back to see if anyone was chasing us.

Decide how important this is and make the first step—put the blinkers on like a racehorse and never to look sideways or back. Not comparing yourself with anyone is not looking back.

> *You should never try to be better than someone else, you should always be learning from others. But you should never cease trying to be the best you could be because that's under your control and the other isn't.*
>
> —John Wooden

Further Reading: *Feel the Fear and Do It Anyway*, Susan Jeffers; *Benjamin Franklin*, Walter Isaacson; *Getting Things Done*, David Allen.

6

NECESSITY

*There are the things you think you need to have
before you can have your dream and there are the
things that hold you back from making the first step.*

THE PROBLEM IS WE GET BUSY with urgent *unimportant* things like paying that bill, washing the car, buying shit, instead of those *important* non-urgent things like writing the book, or taking a few steps towards your dream business. Always keep your goal in mind. Like a pilot adjusting the course towards the destination in the face of the wind or turbulence, you need to always keep your goal in mind.

EVERYTHING IS TOUGH AND EVERYTHING IS POSSIBLE

I was on the train from Bratislava to Vienna, lying under a pile of scrap metal, silently waiting. As I heard the border guards approaching, one of the other guys stowed away with me started coughing painfully. We eagerly shushed him but he still gave another couple of coughs. I was just hoping these would not be heard and he would stop. It made me recall those horror movies where an actor makes an unexpected noise right at the time of the biggest danger and gets caught or killed. Now I was experiencing it in reality. His coughing stopped just as a torch beam passed over us, and the guards left. Luckily, we'd got through, but had to wait a little longer before starting to uncover ourselves.

Right after the train began pulling away from the border, the desire to come out from under the metal was intense—it was as if you were being drowned, desperate to come up for air. The metal had pressed hard into every part of me, and I had a car wheel on my head, which numbed me to the point that I could not move. I hoped that the guy we'd arranged would uncover us all OK. If he was in any trouble, we could be stuck there until who knows when.

We needed to start uncovering soon after we pulled away from the border check so that we were ready to jump off shortly before arriving at the main station, as the train slowed down. I was waiting but couldn't hear the guy that was supposed to be uncovering me. He must have got trapped too and could not get out. I could not move. We had to get off that train before it reached the station but we were trapped.

When I was younger, I had been taught about God by my grandpa, who was a Baptist and a preacher in his church. He would tell me stories about Jesus, David, Solomon, the Apocalypse, and so on. I would draw illustrations for children books with Bible stories from a very young age.

That influenced me and I was a regular visitor to church every Sunday when I was in my hometown and sometimes in Chisinau when I was at LIRPS. I would recite the Lord's Prayer every night and would often talk to God about my needs and desires. Quite often if my desires were fulfilled or a specific situation would sort itself out, I gave God the credit and thanked him for it. As I grew older, I realised that an apparently bad situation would often turn out to be a good one, so I began asking God not so much for things I desired but for things that would be good for me. I have a slightly different view on this now, although I do believe there is an energy that surrounds us and is within us—people may call that God.

While under the scrap metal in the wagon as the border guards approached, I started talking to God, asking him to get me out of this situation—the worst I'd faced in my life. If I could get past this one, I would be sorted and I promised to become a better person. (Well, that is what we all say when we are in trouble, I guess.)

Suddenly I heard a voice talking to me and metal clanging sounds. The guy was starting to uncover me. Apparently he had also been trapped by the metal on top of him and had only just managed to escape. I then learned that the guy who had been coughing had been doing so because a piece of metal had been pressing sharply into his ribs. Somehow, we all managed to uncover ourselves just as the train slowed down before the station, jumped off and headed towards the field.

I saw we were in the woodland that I'd been told about. I had never felt so free before. It was a crossroads in my life, where I could head towards Italy, France or any other

European country. My imagination went wild and I was thinking about these things as if I wasn't on foot but on a plane. Everything felt so close and reachable and that by the end of the night I could be anywhere I desired to be.

There were five of us now—we'd been joined by two guys from another wagon. None of us knew each other from before and we were all like hunted rabbits, our eyes sparkling, rapidly looking left and right, ready to jump and run in any direction. We set off in the same direction, away from the railway deep into the field, having decided to head towards Italy. Three of the guys were certain which direction we should take and there I saw the problem: all three were pointing in different directions. We didn't have any navigation aids to help us. This was when I first felt a connection with Slavik. He acted in a way known to me and had a lot of common sense. He didn't talk as much as the others and considered his words before speaking.

Due to the lack of reliable means of orientation, we decided to stop and hide for the night in the woods, hoping the daylight would help show us a clearer direction.

GETTING TO VIENNA—ASYLUM

After the police raid on the Vienna apartment where we had been staying, we were taken to the local police station, and then transferred to an asylum centre. It was rather like my boarding school, with a canteen, accommodation, bathrooms, common rooms, office blocks for administration and a leisure place where people could exercise, all surrounded by a tall fence and gate that was closed after a certain hour.

It was a form of relaxed prison, and like in my school, the food was terrible.

We sensed, however, the atmosphere was slightly edgy. We learned there'd been a fight between the Moldovan and Chechen gangs during which one of the Chechen members was killed and the tension was still in the air. It was a good idea to keep your eyes open and be alert just in case.

We were given a room with another six people, which felt rather cramped and like a cheap hostel. We started networking to find out how people went about sorting out legal papers for themselves. Those that got papers easily did not share their stories or say what they told the authorities, maybe because they didn't want others to tell the same story, which might take some of the credibility away. It was hard to judge what story would be best to use. We were due to be interviewed soon, and we needed it to be a good story.

We heard that some guys there escaped from the asylum and went to work illegally or steal car radios in the town. When you were stopped or checked by the police, you could just show your plastic asylum card and they would let you go. The card was valid until the decision about you had been made, which would normally take a long while. The cards were different colours, to indicate what kind of case yours was. Usually cards valid for a longer time were given to families with children. The majority of those families were from Georgia and Chechnya.

I met a Moldovan guy who had been in the centre for a few years and had got comfortable with the lack of choice and plans, probably because all the necessities were provided there for free. Quite a few of these guys had families back in Moldova and I felt quite sorry that they were not moving out or doing something.

Meanwhile, Slavik and I got friendly with some energetic young guys we met there. They were discussing an escape plan and we were keen to join. The day after next, we would jump the fence early in the morning at about 3 a.m., break into a car and drive to Italy. As there were no borders, we could be there in a matter of hours.

Before our agreed escape, I had to attend my interview for being given an asylum card, which was very important. It would act like a sort of ticket to sort out any issues and prevent deportation until my case had been decided. During the interview, I did not come up with the magic story that would guarantee me a long-lasting status in Austria. Instead, I just improvised something. While the staff were lovely, my story was rubbish. I did get the asylum card that would buy me time, but there was no chance that I would be given any status to remain permanently.

The night after I'd received my asylum card, we were set to escape and by now I was fully prepared. We met to discuss and plan it in detail. There were six of us, including myself and Slavik. We were the oldest and most mature of all—at nineteen years of age. We agreed that six teenagers all driving in the usual easy-to-break-into-and-steal model of car would be highly suspicious, and pose a high risk for us of being stopped. So we decided to get two cars with three of us in each—Slavik in one car and I in the other. Out of all of us, only two had some driving experience—technically, that meant driving a car a twice without an accident—while three knew how to break in and steal a car.

Around 3 a.m., we jumped the fence and waited for the guys with the cars to arrive. Luckily, they'd chosen ones with a lot of fuel in the tank. We had no phones or means of contact, and did not want to attract unwanted attention, so we agreed not to follow each other but overtake every other mile to stay in touch. The guys felt quite excited. We set off like gangsters, with the music playing loud and driving fast, which was less than reassuring considering this was only the fourth time behind the wheel for the driver! Before we reached the motorway, the car stalled twice, and the driver had to start it again by joining the two wires. As soon as we reached the motorway it felt OK—probably because none of us had any idea about driving.

We were so happy to be on the road and that we would soon be in Italy, where everyone had a plan. Slavik and I would go to his uncle to get shelter and work, and the other guys had similar arrangements. As we were overtaking the other car, we would laugh and wave to each other. The next time we passed the others, they were at a petrol station so we slowed down to give them time to overtake us, which they did shortly afterwards. The next time we saw them, their car was parked on the side of the road surrounded by police and all of them were in handcuffs. Such a shame as they were so close to the border. Not long after, our car was also pulled over by the police and we were arrested, handcuffed and taken to the police station. But it was an *Italian* police station.

It was difficult to understand what police were saying, not knowing the language, but they knocked us around every now and then, which made the point. They would kick one of us on the backside or leg, or give us a slap to the head or face—not very brutal but strong and sharp. We had heard about Italian police brutality towards foreigners and that they weren't nice compared to the Austrian policemen. When the solicitor and translator arrived the kicks and slaps stopped. We created a story that other guys had broken into the cars and given them to us so we could drive to Italy, which I was not sure they believed. They took our fingerprints and released us. We were told that we needed to leave the country in two days otherwise we would be arrested and deported—which I noted quite strongly, as it was the last thing that I wanted to happen.

We were given directions to the train station in the nearby town and headed there. I was alone again and going to Slavik's uncle was no longer an option. Contemplating my next move, I thought of Alex, a guy from my school who had left about six months before to join his father in Italy. I thought I could call him to see what options he had. The other option I had in mind was to go to the guy in Rome who could give me €100 to help me continue my journey. The initial €500 I'd been sent by my elder brother, Alex, was now down to less than €100.

We had been walking towards the train station for more than two hours and evening was approaching. Of the many cars passing by, none had any interest to pick us up when we put our arms out. We were going through the middle of some woods and there was still no sign of a town. It was about midnight or later when we finally entered the town. We reached a shop that was still open, so I decided I would buy a loaf of bread to put something in our stomachs. The guys wanted to smoke so they were pitching to buy some cigarettes. I thought at the time how powerful this addiction was—although starving, they would choose to smoke instead of eating. We gathered the coins we had and bought a pack of cigarettes and some bread rolls, which we consumed rather fast. The others puffed away, with pleasure on their faces.

We had to find where the station was and most importantly, a place to sleep before we could get a train in the morning. It was rather chilly so we walked around to find some shelter, or perhaps meet someone who would give us a place to stay for the night. It was a small town and it did not take long to see most of it. We noticed the church and went to knock at its door. There was no answer so we walked round it in search of shelter. We came across what looked like a nursery, as it was surrounded by a kind of playground. The doors were open so we went in. It turned out to be an abandoned nursery. We managed to find some planks to lie on, and even something to cover us, and went to sleep. Although I was tired, it was an alert type of sleep. I knew we had to be at the train station early in the morning. I didn't want to waste even a minute of my "legal" two days in the country.

When we woke up, we headed straight for the station, which was not far away. When we reached the station there was a great surprise—Slavik and the other guys were also on the platform. I was so happy to see them and we gave each other a great hug—I had the feeling I had known the guy for years and by now referred to him as a good friend. We thought that the other group had been arrested by the

Austrian police just *before* the border, while we had made it across into Italy. However, they had been held in a nearby Italian police station too and were released just an hour before us.

Slavik proposed we should go to his uncle in Verona and maybe settle there as he had a flat and job. We took a train to Verona, with a change in Venice. The other guys were planning to go to their relatives in Milan and Verona, so we all went in the same direction. We looked rather suspicious together so decided to travel in different compartments. We stayed vigilant and made sure we got off in Venice and caught the Verona train. Once on board, we could see the other train from our window. The other guys were still on the train, looking out from the window. We were not clear whether they decided to go further or had not realised that they needed to change. We were sure they would be OK in the end.

Verona station was a building of beautiful architectural quality. As soon as I arrived, I felt the energy of the city, with lots of people going in all directions and the might of the architecture we were surrounded by. The sun was up and the weather was warm and beautiful. Slavik called his uncle and informed him about our arrival. We waited a few hours until he was able to meet us. His uncle had been in Italy for a while now. His family were there, with two young daughters, one at school and already speaking mostly Italian.

At their apartment, for the first time in a long while, I felt a homely type of energy—comfortable, pleasant and caring. That night felt as if it was my best night ever, sleeping in a proper bed with clean sheets. It felt completely amazing—nothing had felt better than that moment. A wave of pleasurable chemistry flowed throughout my body.

The family could not let us stay for long, but Slavik mentioned that he had another uncle who lived in a nearby town, whose name was also Slavik. He was not married and might have space for us, so we decided to head that way. In the morning, we took the train to Slavik's uncle who was already expecting us.

Slavik and his uncle had kept in touch with each other but hadn't met for a long while, so they were really happy seeing each other. It was pleasing to observe their reunion. Uncle Slavik had a room in a large four-bedroom house—at least it looked that way at the time. He had no legal papers and was working as an assistant for a chef and waiting to gain legal status. There was a rule at the time that meant that if you had been working for five years, you qualified to gain legal papers—a *permesso di soggiornio* (a permit to stay). So nephew Slavik also decided that this would be a route for him. Uncle Slavik was a great guy and very kind. He would go to the kitchen and make us some food every day before he would go to work. And he would prepare dinner for all of us when he returned.

I still had the UK in my head and did not feel like stopping in Italy. A friend who was already in the UK had heard about some guy from Lithuania trafficking people using forged Lithuanian passports and driving them from Belgium to London. In order to make that move, I had to get to Brussels. This was the opportunity I wanted and I had to make it happen. I started envisaging all the ways I could do it—starting from a little town in Italy with under €100 in my pocket and getting to Belgium and then the UK. I decided to visit the guy in Rome to pick up the €100 and with the other money that I had left, and some improvisation, perhaps I could reach Brussels. It is strange to look back at that situation: I had so little money, no one around who would give or lend me enough money to keep me going, and no legal papers that would let me receive a money transfer, even if I found someone.

By the third day of me staying with Slavik senior and junior, I managed to conjure an idea that would move me forward. I called my brother Alex, who found the Lithuanian trafficking guy through a friend of mine from LIRPS. Alex, who was working in London, borrowed some money and agreed with the Lithuanian guy to pay him on my arrival. All I needed to do now was to get to Brussels without being caught. I made some passport pictures and sent them to Alex for the fake passport to be prepared.

After the three days, I had to say goodbye to the Slaviks and head to my next destination: Rome. I grabbed my backpack and Slavik and I had a nice forty-minute walk to the station, surrounded by Italian nature, which I'd begun to love. Slavik gave me all the change he had left, which was really kind of him. I gave him my sports costume—the one I wore as a change of clothes. We were of a same size and he liked it a lot so it was a good gesture in return.

Heading to Rome

The train journey to Rome was pleasant. I was staring out of the window the whole time, admiring the views of the countryside—although the fear of being caught never left me.

I met the guy with the money soon after I arrived in Rome and once he'd given me the cash I thought to go straight to the station and catch a train to Brussels. The Rome train station was full of so many foreign people—I could hear Russian, Romanian and Ukrainian, as well as my own Moldovan language, being spoken. As I was waiting someone approached and greeted me in Moldovan. We started talking and I recognized him—he was also a judoka and we'd participated in the some of the same tournaments. His name was Kesha and he suggested I stay for couple of days so he could show me Rome, which I thought was a good idea as I never been there and could use the opportunity to explore this beautiful historic city. I told him my situation and that I had to be very careful not to get deported and that my plan was to reach the UK.

If I'd known how this would turn out, I would definitely have boarded the Brussels train right away....

He first took me to show where he lived and said that he would also introduce me to Rome's *polozhenec* (Russian slang for the gang leader). Kesha said he was a Moldovan guy who was really tough—a sambo expert who'd won a number of cage fights—and a friend of his.

Where Kesha lived was two relatively large buildings, which he said were former schools that had been abandoned and were now full of Moldovan immigrants. And a large Moldovan flag hung out of one of the windows down the side of the building facing the road.

We went into the building where Kesha lived. The former classrooms were divided into five or six little "rooms" with partitions of plywood and curtains hanging instead of doors. The corridor of the building was dark as there was no electricity in the building, but there was water so people were able to drink and shower. It reminded me of our LIRPS accommodation with dark corridors, open toilets and basic washrooms. There were mostly men living there—a mixture of people of a variety of ages, young to old, and a variety of jobs, but mostly low paid, either building or cleaning. Others made their money by stealing and selling the goods locally or transporting and selling them in other EU countries.

He showed me his "room", which looked more like a homeless man's temporary shelter, but there was a mattress covered with some sort of bedding. In the other rooms lived his co-workers. These were guys he went to "deals" with. I understood they were not working on building sites and not financiers either. They began discussing which areas they would cover that evening.

They covered many subjects. How the motorcycle they stole the week before had arrived in Moldova by van. How they stole cars and as they didn't have anywhere to store them, they would just park them in another area of town until they found a buyer. Sometimes those cars disappeared from where they'd been parked, and there was some discussion about what happened to them. Then there was the story

about the guys that had left that week after breaking into a
house and finding a safe full of money. And then the feast
last night with all that nice food and lots of ice-cream. A
group had robbed a restaurant and brought back food for all
to eat—they had also been hoping for a safe full of money,
but it turned out it was not in the restaurant so they filled
their car with food instead.

After the stories had ended, Kesha offered to take me
to see the *polozhenec*, who was based in the other school
building opposite. Everyone there knew and feared him as
the tough guy he was—the head of the underpaid, under-
privileged people.

The *polozhenec* would walk through the school to see
people and they would hand him food and all kinds of
presents in order to get his appreciation and protection.
Occasionally he would punish someone that did not have
enough connections, which served as a confirmation not to
mess with him.

The second building looked a lot cleaner and I didn't see
any people living there. We walked to the first floor toward
the *polozhenec*'s room where a couple of older women were
sorting through some food supplies in their bags. The room
looked more like an apartment and had some of the furniture you'd find in a normal house, which I hadn't seen in
the other rooms. We went past the living room through a
corridor and to his bedroom.

A large guy was lying on his belly with nothing on but
shorts. His head faced away from us towards the TV, which
was showing non-stop porn. A skinny, older-looking guy
was massaging one of his feet.

We greeted him as we entered the room and stood there for a little before he gave a slight turn of the head to acknowledge us. His name was Gosha and we began talking. After we established that I was from LIRPS like him and had done my judo training under Luca, his face soon softened and became friendly.

It could have been because of the types of activity and standard of life they were leading, but they were constantly on edge. I think they did not realise they were living in constant danger—even their typical evening activities were a danger. They never paid for anything, but to me this looked like they were constantly running and constantly under threat—especially given that I was super concerned about having my fingerprints taken and the threat of deportation.

For example, Gosha and Kesha decided we should go to the beach, which was on the other side of Rome, so we'd have to take the train. It sounded like a nice trip and it probably was for them, but for me, with my extra safety and anti-deportation concerns, I was on edge at every step we took.

To travel by train, we would jump the barriers and go on to the platform where we would have to stay by the entry doors to watch for the conductor. If he got into the train, we'd jump out and wait for the next one to take us to our destination. Once we reached there, if there was no fence that we could jump to get out on to the street, we would just run out and jump the barriers again. Every one of these moves was accompanied by a cold shiver through my body, as my mind was concentrating on the threat of deportation.

When we did reach the beach, I was surprised to find it was surrounded by a fence and that you had to pay. Of course, we jumped over it and when the beach inspector came after us we just ran into the sea.

After having a nice swim, we went to a concert hall located by the beach. We'd heard music coming from there, so we decided to check it out. A dance competition was on, so we watched for a bit.

We had a nice time, if you didn't mind the edgy bits running from all sorts of conductors and inspectors that gave me cold shivers. We were heading towards home and feeling hungry when Gosha offered to get some pizza from the takeaway place we just passed.

It was a small shop, maybe eight square metres, with the main counter right in front as you walk in with a lady waiting for your order. On the side behind a glass window, there were roast chickens rotating on spits.

Gosha asked us to go in and ask what types of pizzas they did, and so on. We walked in and Kesha began talking to the lady asking her in broken Italian what type of pizzas they had.

The whole time we were together, we would tell jokes and remind one another of life in Moldova and recount funny stories from judo training or tournaments. Gosha would talk to the locals with a serious authoritative face asking them for directions in his own "Italian" made of Russian swearwords, which was funny as hell. He also would go into a shop to buy eggs and as he wouldn't know the word for eggs in Italian (or perhaps he was just playing his usual games), he would mime a chicken showing the eggs coming out of his butt. Every step of the way, we had laughs....

It was exactly in this same manner that we were chatting to each other and the girl at the counter, when I noticed out of the corner of my eye that Gosha had come in and in a flash grabbed one of the rotating chickens from behind the glass and disappeared. The girl walked towards the door to see where he went but he was nowhere to be found.

As I was lightly paranoid, a cold shiver went through my body again. *Shit, if she realises we are together and calls police or anything like that, I am fucked.*

She didn't and soon the three of us were standing on the side of the road munching on that cooked chicken, ripping it apart like jackals with their prey.

As we finished, Gosha mentioned that he would like to eat some fruit. I got the shivers right away—I knew it would be another incident. I had been on so often about my two legal days and my papers that they didn't mind me not participating in these "incidents". Instead they went into the shop and came out within a couple of minutes with a watermelon and some apples.

On the way home, Kesha proposed I come with them in the evening for a "job", but I decided against it.

I stayed at Gosha's place that night, in the building with electricity. We talked about LIRPS, judo and guys we knew in common. As he was older than me, we had not interacted back in school but we had the same coach, had met at tournaments and had lots of mutual friends.

In the morning, I heard a couple of Moldovan ladies of about forty bringing bags of food supplies like rice and pasta, which they picked up from the "point". The "point" was a place where the government gave out food to those in need, so these ladies (and most of the people living in the two buildings) went there on an almost daily basis. I heard Gosha asking them why they hadn't brought any oil and they answered that it was not being given out that day. I guessed that this was all to do with protection favours and gifts. And I was beginning to notice a hierarchy within these buildings.

Kesha came to inform Gosha that there would be some food "income" today from someone who'd robbed a restaurant. It was clear that Kesha was Gosha's pair of eyes in the other building.

That day, Kesha explained to me that there were two *polozhenecs* "in charge" of Rome. In the criminal hierarchy, the *polozhenecs* would gather valuables and money and send them to the heads of the organisation in prisons across the former USSR. When these *polozhenecs* asked for things, they would be speaking on behalf of the "important" inmates who were pulling the strings from inside prison. This set-up had been extremely influential in the 1990s within the former USSR. They would appoint people who would collect money or do criminal activities on behalf of the big heads in prisons. They had a specific jargon called *fenya*, which was designed to confuse police surveillance, and had created a common budget called *obschak*, which acted like a social criminal financial structure. However, more recently, most people in the former Soviet republics had become more aware, and these old tricks would only work on helpless people who did not have protection and the power to defend themselves; or who had been brainwashed and were too afraid to call the police—in case the police were with the criminals (which was less frequently the case as time went by). One of these *polozhenecs* was Gosha and the other one was Misha—not a friendly guy, Kesha said.

I spent the day hanging round the Moldovan buildings and later in the afternoon the guys organised a barbeque and we had some beers while the sun was shining nicely.

That evening, I learned from Kesha that the *polozhenecs* were building a good team of boys to do some serious deals and that I would be a part of the team. The plans were already prepared and there were opportunities to earn good money. He also said that Misha had insisted I should join and I had to give an answer by the morning.

One of the reasons I'd run away from my country was for a change for the better, but another one of the reasons was to be away of these types of organisations. I had seen this kind of indoctrination they were trying on me back in Moldova and I knew that I would have to disappear from here as soon as possible if I wanted to fulfil my plan to reach the UK. "As soon as possible" meant almost right that minute, as the more time I spent with them, the more chance I'd get involved.

I almost instantly told Kesha that I was not interested and was planning to get a ticket to Brussels the next day.

I knew I had to get away at any price. I did not know what was in these people's heads and what exactly their plan for me was, but I felt the discomfort in the air, the looks, the whispers. Everything created a gut feeling that prompted me to be cautious.

Go, Go

The next train to Brussels would go the following day so I planned to be at the train station in the afternoon.

The evening before I was to leave, I joined Gosha in the building with no electricity. The corridors were dark with the only light coming from a couple of windows. The whole building was buzzing—I guessed it was the end of the working day. The bathroom was full of people, mostly women, washing their clothes. People were knocking on other doors asking for salt, potatoes and other foodstuffs.

The police would often come looking for someone, so it was the common culture that if anyone noticed the police coming they would notify everyone else by making a noise or shouting. Also the windows of the rooms had metal bars and those guys that were doing illegal activities had sawn through one end of the bar so it looked as if it was in place but you could push it aside and jump out of the window if the police arrived. These types of "protection" were common in these communities and people would help each other with little daily things to maintain their important social relationships.

Gosha would walk into the rooms almost without knocking and as soon as he got in, he would ask how much money the people had gathered for him—or rather for the *obschak*—and if there was no money, at least what food they could give. (Everything that was gathered supposedly would be sent by van to the heads that were imprisoned in Moldova or to those in need.)

I realised that all of those he visited seemed vulnerable and hardworking. They'd be perhaps at a construction site or doing some other manual labour, and be middle-aged or older men who were most probably gathering funds and provisions for their own families. It disgusted me that they would have to give part of their hard-earned money to these strong young men. Also, the protection they were buying would only be up to a certain level. If there was a real problem, they would only be helped in proportion to what they were paying. The problem here was the perception of the amounts given: although for those working in low-paid jobs the amounts were relatively large, most of the time by the gang's standards they were small.

Gosha also mentioned the big plans he and Misha had, and that they wanted me in the team, and that it was a great opportunity to generate some good money. He also brought up that it was Misha who had insisted on me joining and I would best give an answer by morning. This passive psychological pushing was getting too much now and I began to feel the need to escape while they were still using a friendly tone. I knew I had to make the train the next afternoon otherwise I could be trapped.

When Gosha finished the round, he ended up with a bag full of money and all kinds of food. I guessed that was another part of the theatre, a bit of a selling technique to show me what life could be like if I decided to stay.

It was already quite late when we joined the guys back at the barbeque. I was approached by Misha who had had a few drinks and was ready to have a "conversation". The talking got more real. Misha said I had no choice but to stay in Rome and be a part of the team that would achieve amazing results. He would come to see me the next afternoon so we could discuss the plans.

This prompted me to "get on my horse" even quicker than planned. I had to get away from this place before I would have to earn my right to choose through some sort of fight, which was not on my wish list.

The next morning, I wished farewell to Gosha and Kesha and told them one more time that staying was not part of my plans and to avoid any confrontations, I would go to the station today. I wanted to be out of Rome by the afternoon, before Misha came by to speak to me. I had no desire to see what was going to happen or what he might try to do. I had to be out of the city. And it was also time for me to go....

There were no trains to Brussels during the day. And the one due in the evening also was delayed and there was a chance that it would not come at all. I had to make a decision. I called my friend Max who had joined his father in Milan. I thought perhaps there would be a train that went there in the early afternoon and I could take the Brussels train from there.

The last time I'd spoken to Max was about four months before and he was fine—his father had got legal papers and Max was able to travel as his son. I gave him a call and asked if I could crash at his place while my papers were being prepared. He said that there were few difficulties with that, but agreed to meet me. He was not exactly in Milan, he added, but would come to pick me up when I got there.

I looked at the train schedule. There was only one train going to Milan that afternoon and it left about twelve-thirty, which I thought was perfect. I decided to buy the ticket and get out of Rome and away from potential trouble. The trouble was it was a Sunday, there weren't many trains running and all the standard class tickets had been sold and there were only first-class tickets left.

I decided to get a ticket anyway so I paid for first-class and informed Max about my timings. I was ready to go, but there were still a few more hours before the train departed, which would be slow going—enough time for me to think about the financial side of buying a first-class ticket. It didn't look great: the €100 I came to pick up from Rome was gone just to cover my travel back. Damn!

During the time before the train departed, I walked round the station. One area looked like Chisinau back in my country—lots of Moldovan people who had either sent or received stuff from the home country. They were sitting round drinking Moldovan beer in small gatherings. These kind of places were ideal for the gangs too, as these people were easily influenced by their dirty tactics of intimidation.

Playing Along

I'd never travelled first class. It was comfortable and felt quite pleasant. The staff were very polite and we were served food and drinks.

But just as I was relaxing after the meal, the shivers came again. I heard a voice over the PA announcing the *polizia* (police) were coming. I immediately thought about the worst-case scenario and my body prepared for action. I began imagining the police passing by checking passports and I was running through the options in my head, although there was nowhere to hide or run to so the options weren't exactly plentiful, especially since my asylum card had expired a while ago .... Then the cleaners arrived. *Pulizia* (cleaning) was in progress after we had finished our meals!

I was looking forward to seeing Max again. I envisaged him looking different and changed after living a while in Italy. When we did meet at the station I saw that nothing had changed, not even his T-shirt, which was faded by the Italian sun. But he did have a tired and slightly scared look to him.

Although his father had received his *permesso di soggiornio*, Max still was being stopped by the police every day and asked for papers and had to keep proof with him at all times. Max thought that since I had no papers, it would be dangerous for me as I could be asked for papers at any time. As I had learned from being in Rome, the key was to look confident and not be afraid of the police when you pass them or when they see you—otherwise you look suspicious. I had practised it already before getting here, so I was relatively relaxed.

As we walked along the train platform we approached some policemen and Max hastily got his mobile phone out of his pocket and proceeded to talk in a louder than normal voice, babbling some abrupt and unstructured Italian sentences mostly made of words like *si* ('yes'). This linguistic acting I found a bit weird.

The problem with Max having been stopped so often was that he was now terrified of the police, so whenever he would see them, he would grab his phone and start saying Italian words. Frankly, this must have looked suspicious to the police, hence they were stopping him all the time and creating paranoia in him.

From now on, there would be no more stop and search. We would both look confident and continue our conversation, regardless of whether we were passing policemen or not.

Max kindly had a ticket for me and we took a train to the town where he and his father lived.

7

TIMING

REMEMBER THIS: Three... Two... One... Action! Just like a rocket ship launching into space.

Don't hesitate—act, as Mel Robbins writes in her book *The 5 Second Rule*, act fast.

ACT NOW

Read the following slowly: Imagine closing your eyes and hearing your inner voice talking to you. Are you happy with the state of your body? The expression you have in the morning before starting the day? Are you happy with your financial affairs? Do you have enough money to sustain yourself or your family? How do you feel about tomorrow, about the next month or the next year? Do you think the situation will change? How does it feel?

Now try to imagine your ideal scenario. Imagine you are doing something you like doing. Imagine you wake up in the morning to your ideal day. Try feeling the smell of the air, try visualising the room you opened your eyes to, imagine the people you want to be with surrounding you, their voices talking to you. How does this feel?

We live a life of survival accepting what we have and inhibiting our dreams and desires as something unreal and unreachable, something we don't deserve.

What are you prepared to do or what are you prepared to pay for a better life? What are you waiting for?

After leaving my home country, I reached my first destination, Slovakia, and found there were people who had been waiting for months for the perfect timing to cross the border, on the perfect train that suited them perfectly. They didn't have the right goal—the goal is not a comfortable process, it is the destination.

The first day I arrived in Slovakia, the train did not come, so the next evening I went to the same spot again, accompanied by a twenty-one-year-old guy who had come with me from Moldova. He wasn't independent enough, so he needed guidance and support at all times.

The place was heaving with people again. By then I'd understood that would be the case every evening. Some of the would-be migrants had even set up a kind of camp there.

It was the last time I would see the twenty-one-year-old guy. He did not get on to the train I got on and I never heard of him after.

I moved quickly, as soon as there was a sign of a right train. There were two other guys that jumped too. I could hear some whispers telling others not to hop on as there should be no more than three people in the wagon. (Apparently, there was a kind of strategy, which I didn't know about at the time but found out later, but I paid minimum attention to it and hopped on without counting the people.)

Within a matter of less than a minute of whispering, a plan was set and the three of us worked in unison. Again, I was amazed at people's abilities in dangerous circumstances.

The wagon was full of scrap metal—all kind of debris, car parts, pipes, and so on. The metal was in a variety of form, shapes and weight, some were heavy and large, others light. We spotted a car bonnet, which looked like the easiest and most efficient cover, plus, it would be relatively easy to get out from under compared with covering yourself with hundreds of kilos of scrap metal, which might settle and press on you while the train was moving.

All these observations and planning were established in those few moments of whispering. We began to make a plan. We'd wait in silence for the conductors, who knocked the wheels of each wagon with a hammer, to pass by, then we could start covering ourselves while the train was on its way to the border, which should take about fifteen minutes.

We agreed which one of us would go under the easy cover of the bonnet. His job was to cover us after we'd dug a hole in the pile of metal, then afterwards to hide himself. And when neared the destination, he also had to uncover us, as the metal would be too heavy and pressing down on us for us to even move. The important thing was for him to be responsible, observant and thoughtful enough to cover us in a way that we would not be visible when the torchlight shone on us, which frankly wasn't such an easy task for him due to the poor visibility at night. Also he had to make sure nothing happened to him, otherwise, we could be stuck underneath all that metal debris until who knew when. At the same time, we were hoping there would not be any accidents or that, as the train moved on the tracks, the piles of metal scrap would not shift and end up crushing you.

There was only a matter of minutes from the time of hopping on to the wagon, to the time when the conductors would begin walking along the train checking the mechanics were in order. The last conductor would knock the wheels with a hammer, which would signal that the train was to pull off shortly.

Soon after our swift plan making, we were lying on our bellies on top of the scrap metal. For about an hour, workers and the conductors were walking up and down below, but finally the hammer guy passed us, banged the wheels and signalled for the train to pull off.

During that hour, something unexpected and unpleasant happened. The hand supporting my head (like a pillow) was resting on sharp metal that was OK for ten minutes but after an hour it had stopped blood circulating to the hand and numbed it—not to mention the agonizing pain, which felt like lying on a knife. The same thing happened with my wrist and leg. I could not feel or move almost half my body by the end. You could not move during that hour as even the slightest shift might disturb the piles of metal and make an unwanted noise that would alert the conductors. That hour felt like an eternity.

As the hammer guy passed and train pulled away, I was pleased to get up, shake my body back to normal and start digging a hiding place in the scrap, but there was another issue. My hands would not listen to me, and the first five or so minutes I operated like I had prosthetic limbs. We had to move fast before we reached the border checkpoint. If we weren't hidden in time, we would be caught and all our efforts would be in vain.

I didn't know the state of the other guys at the time, but I was sure they were not better than me.

Knees and hands often got jabbed by the sharp metal as I dug a hole through the alloy wheels, car doors and exhausts, so it was rather a challenge. Eventually I managed to dig one deep enough using only one hand and the support of my "prosthetic" one—although I suspect I overdid the depth, just in case. The guy in charge (the one under the bonnet) covered me and the other guy and then himself. We made sure we were all fine by shouting to each other.

Everything happened quite quickly and it wouldn't be long before we reached the border check. However, I was already feeling the heavy weight of the metal pressing on top of me and as the train jolted along the track it was shaking and the cargo was moving dangerously. The scrap was settling and pushing into me. I was pleased that I'd succumbed to my desire to put more stuff over me just in case—enough not to be seen and just enough so I wouldn't be crushed me underneath.

It would take about thirty minutes for the border police to check the train once we reached the frontier. They would carefully check each wagon with a torch to make sure no one was there.

The train was slowing down and I was looking forward to the train being checked so I could push off the metal and stop the pain. At that point, a part of me did not care if I was caught or not, my biggest desire was to get out from underneath the weight and make the pain go away. The rest of me was persuading my body to go forward and not to give up. I was almost there ....

We reached the border and I could hear the chatter of the workers going about each wagon. Soon they would reach our wagon ....

THE TRAIN TO BRUSSELS — DECISION MAKING

I'd left Max in north Italy and was on the Paris train lying on the top luggage bench (as advised by the conductor) and I was seriously contemplating my next move. I had to make a decision and act on it.

First, I had to estimate where I was. I did not know where geographically the train was, but I could guess that by now it was almost a third of the way between the point we entered France and Paris. If I compared the fare I paid for Milan to Brussels and imagined it as a distance, I could roughly estimate where I would need to be to get off the train and still be able to afford to buy another ticket with the money I had left (€50). To be on the safe side, I decided to get off when we were what I reckoned was just over halfway. If I waited to get closer to Paris, there might be no more stops and I would be done.

The next thing was to work out exactly when to get off. That was also not that easy since I had no watch and didn't know the time—also I didn't want to surprise and scare the other passengers by appearing out of nowhere from the luggage shelf. We had passed the French border about midnight and the sunrise was some time ago, which I'd noticed in my alert sleep. (This had been my kind of sleep for a while—the type of sleep that fish sleep in which you are still alert and ready for any danger.) The train was scheduled to reach Paris at midday, so my biological clock, located in the "gut", told me it was time to move....

The best idea was to get off when the train slowed down, and *near* but not *at* a station. It would save me walking a long distance to the next town or station and at the same time it was safer. The train slowed before stopping at a station and also went slowly before it accelerated after pulling out of the station. It would be dangerous to jump out at the station as people could see and report me, or I would just be taken by the railway authorities. If I jumped before the station, the platform would be buzzing with people and I would be seen, so the best way, I decided, was to jump off soon after the train pulled out. It had to be just right distance from the station to make sure no one could see me and before the train had accelerated to a dangerous speed.

For sure, by now my initial plan to pretend I was asleep so the conductor did not ask me for passport had been completely distorted beyond recognition—well, this was a lesson in being flexible and adapting to the situation.

At the next stop, another person got into the compartment, so now all the beds were full. When the train began to set off, I dropped my feet down from the luggage shelf, grabbed my backpack and got ready to move.

I tried not to pay attention to the surprised faces of my fellow travellers who were silently gazing at me more than at each other. I knew I should not look in their eyes, as it might scare them and cause trouble. I pushed my head out of the window to check the distance and estimate the train speed. Everything looked right, so I dropped my backpack out and then squeezed through the window and jumped out.

My rough calculations were quite good—the jump was safe and I didn't break any bones or anything like that.

It was probably not quite as safe as I thought at the time. I later heard of another guy from LIRPS who hid between the carriages of a train that was going to UK from Europe and jumped off at high speed. He sustained serious injuries including a crack in his skull. He asked for asylum in the UK and became a hard-working guy and a successful sportsman.

Given where I landed, there was no way someone could have seen me so I walked along the railway to the station. The ticket to Brussels was €46.40, just below the €50 I had left, which was great—it left me some change for a phone call. I'd made a good estimation and a lucky move.

The journey to Brussels felt quick and secure, as there were no stops until the destination so there would be no checks, which gave me a bit of comfort. There were beautiful views on the route and I stared out through the window the whole way.

I had a number to call when I arrived so someone would come and pick me up. And once I got through, I was told where to wait and that there would be two ladies coming to pick me up.

I recognised the Slavic-looking girls approaching to the meeting point. You could see they were Slavic partly from the facial features but more so by the look in the eyes—they didn't have that relaxed and "I don't care what you think about me" European look. They responded to my sign. "How did you recognise us when we are dressed and behaving to not look Slavic?" they said.

We drove to their nearby apartment where there was another guy and a girl—both with similar goals to me. Our passports were ready and we just had to wait for the next available driver to take us to London. It was estimated to be in about two to four days' time.

Just in case, we began learning a bit of Lithuanian and our new names, dates of birth and signatures, which we practised often throughout the day.

The ladies told us stories about what happened to people who crossed but were not prepared and did not remember their new details—how they were captured at the border and when questioned they could not give their date of birth, name or signature. Apparently, sometimes even the fact that the person did not respond to a greeting in Lithuanian got them exposed and captured. I could not afford to fail. I had come a long way, and also I did not want to leave my brother heavily in debt, so I learned eagerly, which was easy since I have a love for languages.

We just stayed in the apartment and never left, waiting for our turn. The next day, it was the turn of the girl, which left me and the other guy waiting. Then I was informed that my driver was also ready and we would be on our way the next day.

The plan was easy: I'd be driven to a French town near the border where I would travel as a passenger in a lorry, acting as if the lorry driver had just picked me up and was me giving a lift to London or somewhere nearby, so there was no connection between the lorry driver and me. When I arrived at the destination, the money for the trip and the passport would be paid to the driver by my brother.

Soon after I got myself into the lorry, we boarded the ferry that crossed the Channel and were on our way to my dream destination. At the border, I was asked no questions about my identity or anything. I could not believe my eyes. I was in the UK and I was free. I had this happy, warm feeling in my stomach like a light coming from within me.

We stopped in a parking lot not far from Dover, so the person who had organised the crossing could come and pick me up. Before he arrived I had various scenarios of the next steps in my head, including one in which I would just run away to save some money, but as I did not know the arrangement with my brother, I soon chilled. I guess my head was on constant alert, hence the abundance of thoughts.

Although, to be frank, my monkey brain still hasn't stopped, even now as I'm writing and is still working out what my next action should be!

Never wait to be perfect before doing what you want—
start and get perfect in practice.

If Apple had waited to release the best iPhone, they would perhaps never have made the first one.

When we took the opportunity to rent our first high-street office in central London and open an estate agency, we heard about a guy who was a managing director in the area branch of one of the largest estate agencies in the country. He'd worked his way up to that position and was doing a great job. The thing was, he could have opened his own agency for the past fifteen years and never did. We did.

None of us knew a thing about how to operate the agency. Google was our teacher.

We had managers of other agencies threatening to send the police and Office of Fair Trading our way, all to try to close our business. They claimed we didn't have one licence or another, or that we were advertising something that we were not allowed to advertise.

We were still coming to the office every day, learning from every situation we encountered. Every time someone formally dressed entered the office our hearts trembled. *Who could this be and what else are we not doing correctly?*

If a formally dressed person did come in asking for the director or the manager, we would ask why. We would say that the director was not in the office at the moment— although we were both the directors and had no one else working for us—and ask him to leave a message. We would then look on Google to find out what the message was regarding and what we would need to do to fix the problem.

We were taking turns to clean the apartments or sometimes would have to close the office for fifteen minutes to go and clean an apartment or fix some issue and then come back and reopen the office. For years, you would see us carrying folding beds and furniture from one apartment to another or from a shop to an apartment. Only after five years did we have a full team to manage the operations. Now our time is relatively free to deal with other matters. (For instance, to write this book.)

The lessons learned are not to wait until you are perfect, embrace your feeling of comfortless and foolishness—there is no other way to learn anything new.

Our old educational system has engrained into us that failure and the sense of being wrong are highly embarrassing. That approach was perfect for generations of manual workers and labourers, who were in a constant submissive mode.

There is no other way to achieve but through feeling foolish, hungry, uncomfortable and embracing those feelings.

A great person expressed that if you find yourself feeling naked in public, that is a sign that you've started doing something right!

For a few months before Radio W.O.R.K.S. World made the offer to me to become a broadcaster, I was envisaging interviewing amazing people. I guess my thoughts attracted the opportunity and I instantly resonated with it and took it on board. I have not thought for a minute that I don't have any skill in the domain—even though I have a speech difficulty that one would perhaps be embarrassed about.

Only forty minutes after I'd accepted the offer, I received an online call. I was not sure if it was being broadcasted. It was indeed—as my first interview.

The thing was that it was less than an hour since I'd finished a four-hour meeting with Marina Nani, founder of Radio W.O.R.K.S. World. I had never expected the meeting to turn the way it did. Through a series of questions and brainstorming she'd helped me establish the structure of this book, the title and the cover—all in that four-hour meeting. I'd been estimating around four months for that.

Anyway, when I was asked in the interview what the name of my book was, I was still in the all-new-information-digestion mode and went blank on the name of the book. The silence felt endless—I felt that I had fallen into a black hole of mental darkness. Eventually, I managed to find the cover of the book on my phone, which had been sent to me by the designer only thirty minutes before, and finally answered.

The rest of the interview felt similar and I was unhappy with the results. *But, hey, no one will care about me as no one knows me, right?*

Going for it and saying yes to what resonates with you and your passion does wonders.

I had woken that morning with a plan to do some book editing and then go to the office to catch up on some work matters. I did neither but achieved something I would not have believed I would achieve any time soon.

I had started writing this book when I was in prison, left it for six months and then decided to finalize it when one day I sat to read what I'd written—I was tempted to know what happened next to the protagonist. Four years later, I spent about eight months finishing writing it. I had handwritten it all on recycled paper from the office (pages with printed text on one side and blank on the other). Another two years had passed when I met someone who offered to print it for me—I just needed to produce a digital copy. Well, that was a tough request at the time, as I was running my new business and working eighteen-hour days six days a week.

When I got my real passport, I went for my first trip out of the country in ten years. As I drove back through the same customs as when I first entered the UK illegally, it was an overwhelming feeling! I realized that this world could do with a Consciously Blind experiment—it is too hooked up on visual status. I had had to endure months of starvation, sleeping rough and danger the first time I came here, and this time it took me no more than four minutes to cross the border. A brand-new car, clean clothes and a red passport definitely made life easier in this world.

This thought prompted me to call the person who'd offered to publish the book, so I could confirm the offer was still on the table and start writing a digital copy.

I found out the person had died shortly before.

Fuck!

He was the husband of my good friend Karina and surely no other person would consider publishing something I'd written. Still, I decided that I needed to put the manuscript in Word format, and not let any other person die before I give him the opportunity to publish this book.

I was sitting in the hotel lobby editing page seventy of my already digitized manuscript when Marina arrived. In the next four hours, the book was prepared!

"Stop editing, there are special people who do this," she said. "Tell me who this book is for!" Question after question, the book took shape, the chapter outlines were written for the text to go in, like the meat on the skeleton. The same happened with the name of the book... *No One's Business—A Migrant's Barefoot Journey to Millions.* "Millions!" Marina explained. "It will mean an abundance of anything for the reader. Whatever is of value for him: people, money, customers... whatever makes him wake up in the morning. Anything is achievable with the same steps."

She paused. "Do you have a nice picture? OK, send it to me."
Next minute, the job was sent to a guy who designs book
covers and an hour later it was ready. "I love all of it," she
said. "It's so spooky, it's as if I have seen this cover before!"

Yet I just could not remember the name of the book forty
minutes later. I was trying to process all this new information with Marina. I was also overwhelmed seeing my eight-
year-long project finally coming to fruition! This day had
turned from initial plan to nearly finished product and there
was too much going on, which I hadn't digested yet. The
interview went terribly, I felt I was answering every question
with the answer to the previous question. Well, anyway, who
cares—as I said, no one knew me there, so it would just be
diluted in the endless stream of daily information.

As I was just calming down, I looked at my phone and
noticed a number of notifications on my Facebook app. I
normally don't have many notifications and this looked like
very many at once. Fuck! The interview had gone online
and was being shared with my friends, some of whom had
already "Liked" it! Now it was perhaps being seen by my
friends, my employees, and whoever was in my Facebook
"gang". The level of embarrassment and shame had over-
taken everything by now. I could imagine people watching
that interview and laughing at how thick I looked!

If you ever had that dream when you are naked in public
and cannot find anything to cover your private parts... that
was my exact feeling.

I tried to comfort myself with the words I've shared above:
if you feel naked, that means you began to do something
right. It was still too difficult! *Why did I bloody do it?! Now I*

cannot take it back! You cannot unsee what has been seen and unhear what has been heard! I'm fucked! The whole thing wouldn't stop bothering me.

Nick, the guy working with us, turned up for some late work. I shared my pain with him, as things always get better when you talk them over and share them with people. "Man, no one will sit and watch that interview, so don't worry. No one has time to watch you talk, everyone is busy with their shit."

That simple change of perspective eased my state.

Those who matter don't care, and those who care don't matter!

At the time of writing, I have conducted at least ten interviews. And, yes, I am shit, but I am still learning. Also I am sure I am doing things right and it's a matter of time.

Don't wait to be perfect, embrace who you are and go towards your idea or goal!

Don't think of details when given the opportunity of a lifetime, just take it. You will find a way, I guarantee you, as I did every time it came to me.

When my girlfriend became pregnant, I didn't think for a minute that I didn't have a stable income, had zero savings or that we were both illegal migrants without valid passports. I was just happy about the news and sure everything would work out. As long as you are happy and the doing right things, it is just a matter of time!

Statistically, it is known that a person on their deathbed mostly remembers those things they haven't done.

If life brings something to you that resonates with your heart, take it, don't wait to be ready. If you want children, if you want to leave that stressful job, if you want to leave a bad relationship, just do it—you only have one life. If you have a business idea or a blog you want to start, just start today. Commit today.

As you read this last sentence, go and register that domain, make a bet with your friends about losing weight in the next month, make that first not perfect video or article. Just do it now!

In the next chapter, you can read one of the interviews I conducted with an individual whose amazing story will inspire you.

If you would like to share your story, contact me through my blog vadimblog.com.

On my blog, I share routines I've learnt and practised from some of the most amazing people on this planet. There are also details of events and classes that I've participated in that focus on personal transformation, which unleashes the potential and attractiveness of anyone and everyone, regardless of the knowledge or experience they possess.

I am also offering mentorship and at the same time I am being mentored myself.

Why would someone need to be mentored? The best performers in the world have mentors and coaches because that is the only way you can constantly push yourself to a new level.

Why would Real Madrid, one of the best football teams in the world, need a coach? They are best in the world! Well, the best performers of any industry have more than one coach or mentor.

If you are serious about what you want to achieve and if you want to be the best in the world, get a coach or mentor. And when you become better than your mentor, change them!

Find out about mentoring with me at vadimturcanu.com.

Subscribe at vadimblog.com to be the first to receive updates on upcoming books, events and promotions.

THE INTELLIGENT
MIGRANT SHOW

I N *The Intelligent Migrant Show (TIMS)*, Vadim interviews those who managed to achieve success through their work and determination. He hopes their stories will inspire and motivate others to pursue their ambitions.

Below is an edited transcript of one of the interviews, with the amazing entrepreneur originally from Russia, **Sergey Kazachenko**.

VADIM: Good morning, good afternoon, good evening, wherever you are in the world. Welcome to Radio W.O.R.K.S. World. This is *The Intelligent Migrant Show* with your host Vadim Turcanu. Our aim here is to prove that it doesn't matter where you're coming from or what your circumstances are, the road to success is there if you're prepared to take it.

Today, our guest is a true example of why we are here, why we're on the show. His story is fabulous. I was impressed by his story. He went to a foreign country at the age of fifteen with only five dollars in his pocket, and went on to achieve a senior partnership in a global investment bank at a very young age. Welcome, Sergey.

SERGEY: Thank you for the nice words.

VADIM: I was amazed by your story. And, it's not only me, but I think everyone will be keen to find out how this transformation happened and what gave you the strength to do it.

SERGEY: Well, you know the biggest strength is when you don't have any choice—it's the biggest benefit in life. If you need to find out the way forward and you know there's only one way and it's forward, then you just find the way to do it. You keep on pushing yourself until you find the solution for whatever you're aiming to do. And for me it was finding the balance in life. No choice was a big start.

VADIM: That's right, there's no way back. Sergey, what are you doing now? If someone would ask you: "What are you doing, what's your job?" how would you answer?

SERGEY: Well, I'm a professional investor. We invest in real estate, we invest in venture capital, we invest in liquid assets. We help other people to achieve their dreams and success stories—both on the company side, for example, a start-up that wants to develop something and bring it to the market, and the individual, for a person who wants to have a passive income and more freedom. We are providing an opportunity for others, so more and more people can get into the same position as I managed to. If we can make their road faster, we'll be very happy.

VADIM: So who are your clients at the moment? Who is your ideal client?

SERGEY: There are two different clients. Client number one is the start-up, a relatively young start-up that has a good product, a good idea but maybe doesn't have the business expertise or the business knowhow to achieve the success themselves and they need the help. They need to put a strong business structure, financial modelling or marketing and branding behind it. That would be client number one.

The second client is, of course, the private individual that maybe is stuck in their job or has been doing phenomenally well in their professional life, but has not achieved the freedom to do whatever they want and are passionate about. And we provide the opportunity for them to be able to achieve that freedom by investing correctly, safely and securely in the different opportunities out there.

VADIM: You sound very organized and professional at what you do. But how did you to get there? If I hadn't read or heard your story, I would've thought the guy had an easy life and had easily achieved success. How did you come to this position? Can you walk us through your life from the time you moved to a foreign country? Because we have some of our listeners, I think, they don't see a clear road, the way they should go. How did you decide to go into this area?

SERGEY: I started quite early searching for a way forward. I come from phenomenal family in Russia, but it wasn't financially advanced. They motivated me to find my own path from an early age. I think I was twelve or thirteen when I started trying to figure out ways to earn additional money, which I succeeded in doing with my first young entrepreneurial career. That was buying and selling ski equipment, because I was a cross-country skier.

It worked out very well for me, so I started looking at where I could go next to actually get that financial stability that we didn't have back in Russia when I was growing up. For me, the obvious choice was to move somewhere to get that and choosing between two countries that I was familiar with, which were Finland and Sweden.

Sweden looked very appealing, so I started looking at the options to reach out and end up in Sweden. I was lucky enough to compete in different tests and exchange programs and was chosen to go to Sweden for nine months as an exchange student. The funny part of that was that I was supposed to study in Swedish—a language that I'd never heard before my first day in school there. That was a bit of a challenge.

I was supposed to be in Sweden for nine months and then fly back, but I was determined to find a way to stay and continue my studies. So I spent a lot of time learning Swedish quite aggressively. And I actually ended up with the third best exam results out of all the students, and not only in my school, but the whole county. That impressed people and they offered me the chance to stay for some more years. That's how it all started, basically....

VADIM: It wasn't luck, then?

SERGEY: I was partially lucky, but I don't believe luck is something that you get. Luck is something you deserve. And I had to sacrifice a lot of time and effort. And it's not easy to be a new person in a new community. I was the only foreigner in the whole community, a big outsider, and had to overcome the physical challenges, which as a fifteen-year old kid you meet a lot of. But I was lucky there were good people around to support me when needed. Thanks to them I could push through and get that first diploma in high school and go to the university I wanted. I opened my first company when I was seventeen and then I got recruited into the finance world.

VADIM: It started rolling out quite quickly.

SERGEY: Exactly, exactly.

VADIM: Sergey, forgive me, I need to come back a bit. I also decided to change country, and I've been blessed with good people. The secret of meeting good people that you can trust is trusting people and being open yourself. You cannot trust someone without trusting them. You cannot find out that you can trust them until you trust them, you know.

It's not only me, I think everyone who is listening will have the same question, but I want to find out about those competitions that you won before going to Sweden. You talked quite casually without giving any credit to yourself, but I think it's quite important, what made you win the competition, and how did you prepare for it? And what would you advise maybe for younger listeners? What are the keys to the locks?

SERGEY: If you want to go abroad, for example, the big, big support, of course, is a language and some very good practical knowledge. The practical knowledge I had was that I enjoy maths and I'm relatively OK at it. But then the opposite side of that was the language, which I was not particularly great at. To get both, the language and my core skill, together, which are opposites, was a very big challenge.

I ended up spending a lot of hours on extra work after school to study English, which was the language I needed to go anywhere. I spent a lot of hours studying with a private teacher. Well, she was my schoolteacher, but I convinced her to help me improve my English, and for her it was a big blessing because she could showcase somebody who'd spent time and what the benefit of that could be.

It was hours, and hours, and hours and, of course, it was not an easy choice. Friends were out there enjoying other events and activities and stuff like that, and I would be back home doing extra work. I wouldn't say I was studying all my life, that's definitely not the case, but I did put in a lot of hours to get that one thing that I needed right. And it's a lot of effort, a lot of striving to get there. It doesn't come easy.

VADIM: Oh yeah, I know exactly what that means. Sacrifice... you know it's all about the payment for the future, that you need to pay now in order to get your future in order. It's amazing that you didn't know anything about the language in Sweden. How did everything go? How did you manage it?

SERGEY: It was a big challenge. Sweden was good because everyone speaks some level of English, which is great and it's a good starting point to start to communicate. But then when you start talking about studies, at school, of course, they had all their lectures in Swedish. I would come back home around three o'clock in the afternoon and I literally went to bed because my head was spinning from the language, which I'd never heard before and I was supposed to understand something from it. And three weeks later, I had the first exam—it was biology in Swedish, which was a bit of a... you know... I had to pass it to be able to get a good grade, so I literally had to memorise one chapter of the book, letter by letter, to be able to pass the exam. It was quite fun because I didn't know what the answer was, I just knew that the answer was supposed to be long. And that's how I made it.

It was literally physically and mentally very challenging to get a new language and in a couple of weeks to start communicating. But my biggest help was that from day one I joined a sports team. In the football team, you know fifteen people and everybody speaks Swedish around you at practice and when you socialise, and you're forced to listen. Even if you're not good at speaking, you're forced to listen. And you want to be part of it, right? You don't want to be an outsider.

VADIM: That's correct.

SERGEY: That was a big help for me. Definitely.

VADIM: That's a very good observation of yours. When you're learning languages, and other stuff, the more type of information—like tactile, visual and auditory—the better. So I guess with sport, learning the language came with physical involvement as well as the communication side of it.

Sergey, I had this in my head to ask you. My situation was that I had to run away from circumstances, the state I was in. There was starvation, poor people around you, and you yourself didn't have any means. There was no future ahead and the economic situation was so bad. Although, I was an Olympic hopeful, a black belt in judo, and I had success, I literally didn't have anything to eat quite a lot of the time and no money. So one day, I decided I needed to change, and like you did, I needed to go somewhere.

What was your "why"? What was your determination? Why did you decide to go away?

SERGEY: It's very simple. My parents are phenomenal and I'm grateful to them. They're big role models in terms what they've achieved with their lives. And a big challenge for me was looking at them as a kid and seeing that they wanted to give me so much more but they couldn't afford it. I had a great childhood with a good family, but just looking at that devastation in their faces, at some point, you feel that they want to give more but they cannot. And that was the decision. I knew one day I'll have my own kids, and I don't want them to see that expression on my face. I don't want them to feel that way about me. That was a big, big "why".

And I knew that I needed to get that sorted and structured before I had my own family. My parents have given everything to me and my brother and we are where we are thanks to how they raised us. But I just wanted to take what they've taught us to the next level, and financial stability is the next level for me. I never expected to get where I am now and it's been a great blessing. I have my two lovely daughters now and we can spend time together and we can enjoy life and it's a blessing.

VADIM: I'm looking at you and I can see inside such a big fire that doesn't show from outside. And looking at your career, you've gone up and up and up! Looking at those steps, many people would stop at the middle or even lower than that and be happy with what they have at that point, but something in you just strives to go up and up and up. What drives you there?

SERGEY: It's a vision. You know, vision is the keyword to success generally. It's even more important when it comes to us, when we're coming from abroad and we need to do something in a new culture, in a new way, new practical things that we didn't know anything about. The vision is big.

The biggest challenge I've seen for people is that either they don't have the vision or they don't have a realistic vision or they don't adjust the vision they have. To have financial stability, that was my big, big vision and I achieved that earlier than I expected, so at the point I could have been satisfied. But that's not the life of a happy person. Happiness comes not from the result but from the process of achieving your result. And so, the way I see it is that you need to have a vision that is very strong. The vision and the goal should be so tangible that when you close your eyes, you can almost feel it, you can almost literally touch it and grab it, you can smell it, you know the exact details of it. Once you get that together, you start finding the ways, finding the paths towards it. And you realise the challenges that you need to overcome to get there.

The biggest challenge I've seen for people is that they choose, so to speak, to stay at a certain level. Those are people who don't move their targets, don't move their vision, don't create a new one. I think part of a successful life and successful story is that you're actually managing to achieve and put the new vision in place.

VADIM: Those are great words, Sergey. That's always also motivated me. It's a known fact that thoughts become things and when you have a goal, you need to envisage it in a very detailed way. You need to visualise your goal and how you feel, what you'll smell, the tactile, everything… That's exactly how you're explaining it. That's the only way for it to become reality.

If you go back to, let's say, your twenty-year-old self, or maybe even the fifteen-year-old, when you decided to move, what would you do differently? What would you advise from the position you are in now? What would you say to yourself at fifteen?

SERGEY: That's a very, very good question and a very difficult one. Clearly, as you know, you make mistakes in your life, because you're learning. The only people who don't make mistakes are the ones that don't do anything. I've been on many different paths in life and taken different steps, I have visited and lived in many places and met many people, and I think my biggest mistake, if you look back now, is not being as adjustable as you can from day one—especially when you're coming into a new culture.

You don't need to be different person, you don't need to accept everything and change yourself, but you need to accept that people can be different. And cultures can be different, and religion, politics, whatever it might be. You might have a different opinion about it, and that's absolutely fine, that's what creates a society that is interesting and exciting.

For me, the big challenge was to come from a relatively small village in the middle of nowhere with a Russian mentality to Sweden. That was as a big cultural shock as it could probably be. And if I had been more open from day one, I think it would have helped. But I'm grateful that I ended up culturally aware and open now.

I lived in the United States for a short period of time after that and saw many people who were staying in the society, a new society, but they chose not to accept the differences. I'm not saying people have to change—you should always stay who you are, stay with your culture, stay with your roots. For me Russia is a big thing, I am Russian and proud to be so, but you need to realise that there are benefits, pluses and minuses, in any culture, religion—whatever it might be. Just embrace that. Once embraced, the integration will be so much faster, so much smoother. And your own results will be faster and your success will come faster.

My biggest benefit in life has been that I'm from a different culture and I know different languages, things like that, but that's only because I was also able to communicate with my local colleagues on their terms and keep my Russian identity. But if you're just keeping your Russian identity and not embracing the local culture, it would have to be challenging. And I've seen people like that living in Sweden today.

VADIM: That's correct. I understand exactly what you're saying. Sometimes it's hard to change because those ingrown cultural things we preserve in ourselves to survive, in a way—it's our survival mechanism, which is not easily broken. Only when we step out and open ourselves up do other people open up as well. That's when you're gonna see the true people. And it's exactly right that without integration into the community, you can't go far. I completely agree with you.

I think my mistake was to be too busy in my sport, judo—twice a day, six hours a day, for six days a week. What I would advise my twenty-year-old self, even my fifteen-year-old self is to read more. Reading gave me so much, you know, opened up so many angles for me, so many opportunities, so many options. And I am blessed to have opened my eyes in that way.

That was your advice to your fifteen-year-old self, but what about the twenty-year-old? There were a lot of changes, going from fifteen to twenty, a quick step up, step up, step up, a quick development of your personality. By the age of twenty, you already had some of the achievements that people of an older age are still working towards, so what would you advise your twenty-year-old self on how you would make it better? Or if someone now was in your position?

SERGEY: Today, I'm very open and very social, and I see the good in every person I meet, until they prove me wrong. I was not that way when I was twenty. I didn't have that freedom and still had some weight on my shoulders from the things I needed to achieve financially. I think at this moment, when you become more positive about things around you, life becomes easier. And it's not because you changed that much, but you're open and then it's easier to accept things.

When you're positive, it means you've seen the opportunity in everything that happens around you, instead of seeing the limits or the problems. And, I think, with every problem, there comes an opportunity. And with every challenge, there's an opportunity. Looking back, I've had some phenomenal ideas and phenomenal things that I worked on that wouldn't have happened if I hadn't accepted the challenges and problems.

People who are generally optimistic impress me a lot. I am not optimistic by nature. But I became optimistic when I didn't have any weight on me anymore. But I would say that period of time, from twenty to twenty-five, was definitely huge, huge support financially, in terms of having achieved success early.

VADIM: Man, this is great advice, some amazing words. Every business came from a problem. Every business out there is just based on that: Look at the problem, try to solve the problem.

Was there any person that was very pivotal or influential in your life starting from your twenties up until now, maybe a business partner, or your father... somebody that influenced you toward making yourself into a better you?

SERGEY: There are people in my life without whom I would not be here at all. Such as the woman who invited me to Sweden. If she hadn't chosen me out of all the candidates, I wouldn't be here. I call her son "my Swedish brother", and we became very close. Also another friend of mine in Sweden who allowed me to stay with him for a couple of years when I got my studies extended. And he's still a good friend of mine. Without him, I wouldn't be here at all.

Of course, there are business people that I've met, like my first boss at my first job, who actually hired me. That was the funniest interview I think anybody ever experienced in their life. We were sitting opposite each other and my answers were completely wrong, way off, because I didn't have the knowledge for it, and he still gave me a chance. He said if you're brave enough to go for your point and try to convince me and you have the drive behind it, you will be successful one way or another. He said, "I just need to make sure you have the brains to back your boldness." So I am very, very grateful to him for giving me my first shot at the financial world.

As a role model, I think if you asked me, a younger version of myself, I would have got more benefit from somebody coaching me from day one. Somebody that I could have followed and listened to more in detail. That's my advice to everybody: find somebody near you that you can rely on and you can trust. Find somebody you can talk to, express ideas to and that will help you. Unfortunately, I didn't find that person, or, to be honest, there were people around that I could have embraced as my coaches but I was just too naive and thought that I could do it on my own. I've made mistakes that I could have avoided if I had just listened to the right people and had them close to me. But all of those people that I've mentioned, without them I wouldn't be here today.

And, of course, my father is a big role model for me in terms of what he achieved in his life. And every time I've had a challenge or problem, I look back at him and what he managed overcome. At that point, I feel that any problem I have is just, you know, it's nothing.

VADIM: That's correct, it's very important. If you don't have those people, if there is no way you can afford to have such a person or if there's physically no one there that you can look up to, at least now there's the internet, there are books and other opportunities. But the road ahead is to learn from people who are already in that position.

SERGEY: In the new part of my life, the big help has been the coach. I realise now that the coach and mentor are quite important. I have a coach now who guides me through my business world. His name is JT Foxx and he was the one who pushed me out of my comfort zone and forced me not only to accept where I was, but actually push forward and put a new vision in place. He forced me to search and reach for something more, when I was getting a little bit more comfortable than I should. So, I'm grateful to him. If you listen to the people that you meet in your life and embrace the message, it will be substantially easier to get results out of yourself. Yes, a mentoring coach is important. Unfortunately, I've realised that now and not ten years ago.

VADIM: It's good that you've realized it now and not ten years later! It's very important being coached. Let's say eighty percent of the businesses that are started end up in bankruptcy or closing down, but if you look at the franchise businesses, the success rate is eighty percent. It's only because there's a system there, like a mentoring or coaching system, that teaches people and trains them how to do that particular business. And what you're saying is exactly correct: if you have an opportunity to learn from someone who is already there, you've got to use that opportunity—because that's the most successful way to succeed in what you want to do.

Another thing I wanted to share with you, Sergey, you just said something about pushing, that your coach was pushing you when you got a bit comfortable. There's an American businessman Jesse Itzler, very successful, and he was running an ultra-marathon and saw this huge guy, around 120 kilos, who had literally broken every single bone in his feet, but was still running. Jesse Itzler looked at him, thinking, what the heck, who is this guy? He later contacted the guy and said, I wanna meet and learn from you. And he decided in a flash to invite the guy to come to his house for one month to live with him and his wife, just so he could learn from him. And this guy was a Navy SEAL. The SEAL said, well, if you're crazy enough to invite me to your house, I'm crazy enough to accept that.

The SEAL came to Itzler's house and on the first day he got him doing push-ups. When Itzler couldn't do any more, he forced himself to do a few more, and in the end he did about forty push-ups. And then the SEAL said, now you need to do another hundred. What are you saying? said Itzler. I've just given everything I could! No, you need to do another hundred. And the SEAL pushed him to do them. So he slowly did them and he said, I didn't realise I had this strength in me.

What the SEAL was saying was, when we think we've given the most we can that is only forty percent of what we are able to do—if we believe in ourselves. We, literally, leave sixty percent of our potential on the table, if we don't push enough. That's so powerful.

You're blessed to have those people who are pushing you—this person who pushes you, makes you grow and go forward. Amazing.

SERGEY: It's a proven point that you're describing—we're using a very limited percentage of our capacity. And there's a huge amount of people who use even significantly less than that! I do a lot of international speaking to help entrepreneurs and help businesses and motivate people. There's a very good story that my coach used to tell me and I repeat it a lot when I also do speaking.

If there are two skyscrapers and there's a small tightrope between them you need to cross to get to the other side, will you do it? Probably not. If there's a small tightrope to cross and the second house is on the fire, you're definitely not gonna go to the other side. But now imagine the same situation: there's a tightrope to the other side and second building is on fire *but* your kid is on the other side. It probably will never be a problem for you to get to the other side, because you suddenly become partially limitless. And that's why I talk a lot about how to force yourself to rise above your limitation. I had a lot of limitations *from* myself—I put a lot of limitation on myself. Society also puts a lot of limitations on you and it's very tough to try to overcome that. Because we are used to thinking in a box that somebody else put on us, but once you overcome the limitations, that's when the real thing happens. And that's when you find your true self and that's when you achieve different results.

VADIM: So powerful, man. That's exactly right. That's when the magic happens. You don't know what you're capable of until you do it and push, push, push. It's amazing.

How people can find you? If people want to learn about your business, what you do, your services, where would they find you?

SERGEY: Facebook. That's the beauty of social media. It's very accessible. It's by far the easiest way to find me personally. And then all the business opportunities you can find on my personal page as well. And I'm happy to communicate with people who are interested to do something business wise or for personal advice. So Facebook is the easiest way to reach out to me.

VADIM: Let's say someone is willing to invest in some sort of product or looking for ideas—maybe he's got an idea to start a business—at what point should he get help, for example, with budgets?

SERGEY: Moneywise, we are looking at all the options out there. So it doesn't really matter what stage you're at, we will review the opportunity and come back with feedback. If it is not for us, we will recommend somebody. In personal terms, for people who want to find their dream life with freedom— so they can follow whatever their personal passion is—and do it through passive income, we are happy to explain how that can be achieved. Absolutely, without any problems. In these cases, the easiest way to reach out to us is probably in an email. Our email address is post@schinv.com.

VADIM: Thanks, people will also be able to find out about you on our Radio W.O.R.K.S. World YouTube channel and our Facebook page as well.

Sergey, it's been a blessing to learn about your story. You're very inspirational and empowering.

SERGEY: The pleasure is all mine. I've read through your personal biography and I'm very impressed. I'm really happy that people like you are putting things like this together to reach out and support whoever feels they need support. The more people that can benefit from this, the more meaning we can have in our lives. So, I'm very grateful for the opportunity to speak to you today.

VADIM: That's cool, Sergey. I hope to see you soon and wish you all the best with your business and striving towards your goals.

IF YOU WANT TO BE EMPOWERED

see your own potential and overcome self-imposed limits that are stopping you from realising it, an UNCAGE EVENT is the place to go. Through exercises and discussion, we reach a new state that will let you understand yourself more deeply and hear the answers to the questions you ask yourself.

INTERNATIONAL UNCAGE EVENTS

are conducted in different cities across the world, and you will get free entry for one of them (in any country). Just turn up with a copy of this book. To find out more and register for an upcoming event, please go to:

www.vadimblog.com/uncage

ABOUT THE AUTHOR

BORN AND RAISED in Moldova, Vadim Turcanu trained as a judo professional and is a black belt athlete. He loves drawing portraits in ink in his spare time and practising judo with his son.

Endlessly delving into books on self-development and market research, Vadim is a successful entrepreneur who currently co-directs a multimillion-pound property management firm in London.

His greatest aspiration is to offer opportunities to others through his knowledge via mentoring sessions.

Email: info@vadimturcanu.com
www.facebook.com/VadimDTurcanu
www.vadimblog.com

Made in the USA
Las Vegas, NV
30 November 2021

35692750R00100